Discipline
with Dignity

3rd Edition

ASCD MEMBER BOOK

Many ASCD members received this book as a member benefit upon its initial release.

Learn more at: **www.ascd.org/memberbooks**

Discipline *with* Dignity

3rd Edition

New Challenges, New Solutions

Richard L. Curwin

Allen N. Mendler

Brian D. Mendler

Association for Supervision and Curriculum Development
Alexandria, Virginia USA

Association for Supervision and Curriculum Development
1703 N. Beauregard St. • Alexandria, VA 22311-1714 USA
Phone: 800-933-2723 or 703-578-9600 • Fax: 703-575-5400
Web site: www.ascd.org • E-mail: member@ascd.org
Author guidelines: www.ascd.org/write

Gene R. Carter, *Executive Director;* Nancy Modrak, *Publisher;* Julie Houtz, *Director of Book Editing & Production;* Deborah Siegel, *Project Manager;* Greer Beeken, *Senior Graphic Designer;* Mike Kalyan, *Production Manager;* Valerie Younkin, *Desktop Publishing Specialist;* Sarah Plumb, *Production Specialist*

All Web links in this book are correct as of the publication date below but may have become inactive or otherwise modified since that time. If you notice a deactivated or changed link, please e-mail books@ascd.org with the words "Link Update" in the subject line. In your message, please specify the Web link, the book title, and the page number on which the link appears.

ASCD Member Book, No. FY09-2 (November 2009, PS). ASCD Member Books mail to Premium (P) and Select (S) members on this schedule: Jan., PS; Feb., P; Apr., PS; May, P; July, PS; Aug., P; Sept., PS; Nov., PS; Dec., P. Select membership was formerly known as Comprehensive membership.

PAPERBACK ISBN: 978-1-4166-0746-5   ASCD product #108036

Also available as an e-book through ebrary, netLibrary, and many online booksellers (see Books in Print for the ISBNs).

Quantity discounts for the paperback edition only: 10–49 copies, 10%; 50+ copies, 15%; for 1,000 or more copies, call 800-933-2723, ext. 5634, or 703-575-5634. For desk copies: member@ascd.org.

Library of Congress Cataloging-in-Publication Data
Curwin, Richard L., 1944-
    Discipline with dignity : new challenges, new solutions / Richard L. Curwin, Allen N. Mendler, Brian D. Mendler. — 3rd ed.
        p. cm.
    Includes bibliographical references and index.
    ISBN 978-1-4166-0746-5 (pbk. : alk. paper) 1. School discipline—United States. 2. Problem children—Education—United States. I. Mendler, Allen N. II. Mendler, Brian D. III. Title.

    LB3012.2.C87 2008
    371.5—dc22

                                                    2008030843

_____

18 17 16 15 14 13 12 11 10 09 08 07   1 2 3 4 5 6 7 8 9 10 11 12

I dedicate this wonderful book to my wonderful family:
The Garber clan
  Esther Garber (1881-1966)
  Joseph Garber (1884-1948)

  Ann Curwin (1908-1987), Mollie Hurwitz (1906-2002),
  Al Garber (1914-1998), and Mickie Ellison

  Mimi Berkley (1941-2001), Jane Mason, Diane Ginsberg,
  Kenny Garber, Steve Garber, Joyce Curwin,
  and Elliot Curwin (1932-2003)

Rick Curwin

 To my wonderful children, Jason, Brian and Lisa, my awesome
daughter-in-law Ticia, and my precious grandchildren, Caleb and Ava.
You are what has truly given meaning to my life. To my wife, Barbara,
for your love, support and lifelong friendship. And finally, to my
lifetime friends, John Bulger, Martha Bulger, Susan and Howard Itkin,
Marty and Jan Krupnick, Linda Steinberg, and Patty and Scott Tripler
for growing old together and being there through thick and thin.

Allen Mendler

To my mother, Barbara Mendler:

Thanks for your constant support, guidance, advice, and love. Your
dedication to our family and to the students you taught are traits I
can only hope to one day copy. I love you.

Brian Mendler

Discipline with Dignity

3rd Edition
New Challenges, New Solutions

❧ Preface ❧

When ASCD asked us to write a new edition of *Discipline with Dignity*, we were given an opportunity to review our work and its impact on children in the years since we first wrote it. We invited Brian Mendler to join us in this endeavor. Brian is an experienced teacher and has used the Discipline with Dignity strategies and philosophy in his classroom with the most challenging of students. Brian adds real-life experience and fresh ideas to our original work. He has challenged us to review our older beliefs and brings a wonderful charm that has greatly enhanced this new book. We are very grateful for his contribution.

Throughout the process of writing this book, the three of us have carefully examined every page of our original work. We are happy to say that much of the original work is still pertinent and remains intact. However, we have enhanced, added, and learned so much since the first publication. Students have changed, society has changed, schools have changed, and, of course, so have we. This edition stays true to our original beliefs and values. Children and teachers need dignity and tools to learn to become responsible people. Yet so much more has been added. We hope you benefit as much from reading this new edition as we have from writing it.

Notes

Gender

We felt uncomfortable with the convention of using singular masculine pronouns like *he* and *his*, so we have tried to alternate between *he* and *she* throughout the book.

Voice

Throughout the book, we use the plural *we* for our thoughts, ideas, and strategies. We have also included personal stories and anecdotes. We have purposely left out the name of the author who experienced the anecdote.

Rick Curwin
San Francisco, CA

Allen Mendler
Rochester, NY

Brian Mendler
Rochester, NY

❧ Acknowledgments ❧

The authors wish to acknowledge and thank the following people for their contributions to our work and to the writing of this book:

—Jon Crabbe, Allison Yauchzee, Kassy Gallup, and Jennifer Beyor, for their day-to-day work at the Teacher Learning Center. Our busy and hectic lives are not possible without you holding it all together. Thanks for all of your hard work.

—Jeannette LaFors, Envision Schools, City Arts & Technology High School (San Francisco), Josh Brankman, Principal, Metropolitan Arts & Technology High School (San Francisco), Glenn Dennis, Principal, Envision Academy of Arts & Technology (Oakland), Karen Wolff, Principal, Impact Academy of Arts & Technology (Hayward), and Jen Davis Wickens, Principal, for allowing us to visit their classrooms and learn from their teachers and programs.

—David Curwin, Andrew Curwin, and Daniel Curwin, for their invaluable research and Internet searches.

—Jessie Vance, Peggy Holtman, Claudia Weaver, Cheryl Clancy, and Pat Yahle at the Milwaukee public schools, for their collaboration in a major project to reduce suspensions and detentions in the district. We learned a great deal from this collaboration.

—Barbara Dorff and Bob Schmidt, Green Bay Area Public Schools (WI).

—Paula Gianforti, Director of Special Services, Gananda Central Schools (NY).

—Michael Pfister, Superintendent, South River New Jersey Public Schools.

—David Triggs, CEO, Academies Enterprise Trust (UK).

—Susan Goode, Director of Curriculum, Meadville Public Schools (PA).

—Bill Osman, Supervisor of Professional Development, Mentoring & Character Education, Hamilton Township Public Schools (NJ).

—Sarah Greer, Teacher, Peru Central Schools (IN).

—Becky Zelesnikar, Teacher, Greece (NY).

—Mary Hawk, Principal, Meigs Middle School.

—Chris Epperson, Coordinator of Special Programs, Fayetteville (AR) Public Schools.

—Renee Carroll, Principal, Batavia Schools (OH).

—Pamela King, Principal, Jones Jr. High School (OH).

—Victoria Shepardson, Director, Cayug a-Onondaga Teacher Center (NY).

—John Freeman, Principal, Pittsfield Elementary School (NH) .

—Cheryl Adams, Staff Development Coordinator, Wausau, WI.

—Sharon Gray, Coordinator Department of Curriculum and Instruction, Virginia Beach Public Schools (VA).

—Project DARE, Portsmouth, NH.

—Diane Taylor, Safe Schools Coordinator, Chicago, IL.

—Michael Gersch, Deputy Executive of Special Education, Staten Island Integrated Service Center, Staten Island, NY.

—Fisher Middle School, San Jose CA.

—Dr. Pamela Wolfberg, San Francisco State University, for her suggestions on autism.

—Dr. Sid Simon, University of Massachusetts.

—Marylin Applebaum, Applebaum Training, for her great suggestions.

—Carolyn Poole, Scott Willis, Deborah Siegel, and Nancy Modrak of ASCD, for their invaluable assistance and superb editing.

—Vicky Cook, Antioch College.

—Paul Montanarello, Principal school #36 Rochester NY.

—Teacher Learning Center Consultants: Jerry Evanski, Dave and Colleen Zawadzki, and Willeta Corbett for their outstanding skills in providing discipline and motivation seminars based upon our work.

—Dr. Phil Harris, for being a great educator and friend.

❧ Introduction ❧

Jack Hasselbring, a music teacher who attended one of our recent discipline seminars, commented, "I really value your ideas on discipline, especially during a very tough first year of teaching at an inner-city school. I was given your book and a taped seminar of yours, and it saved my career." At the same seminar, a young lady asked us, "I've heard of Discipline with Dignity, but I do not know what it is. Can you tell me?" Between these two incidents lies the reason for this newly revised edition of our book *Discipline with Dignity.*

This special edition of *Discipline with Dignity* is a thank-you to the thousands of educators who have gratified us by learning and using the concepts and strategies from the first two editions to benefit students and make their schools better places. Unlike the second edition, in which we added a new introduction but kept the original book intact, this edition offers new insights, concepts, and many updated strategies and interventions to help educators facing the greater challenges of today's youth.

It is not easy to give a simple answer to the question "What is Discipline with Dignity?"

- It is not only a program.
- It is not just a solution.

• It has a structure that can apply to all situations, but it is not a standardized formula.

• It does not change children to be somebody else. It makes them better at who they already are.

We define this approach as a set of values on which interventions, strategies, and constructs are built to help children make informed choices to improve their behavior and to make life better for teachers. When that happens, children are so much more likely to learn the content we want to teach, understand why they need to learn it, and comprehend how to use it in constructive ways to improve their lives and the lives of others.

Much of what we introduced in the first publication of this book was considered radical then but is now accepted as good practice by most educators. The ideas of students helping develop rules and having a say in choosing a consequence are examples. Defining discipline as teaching responsibility rather than simply demanding obedience is another. In fact, if imitation is the sincerest form of flattery, then the number and variety of programs that have adapted, borrowed, and used the Discipline with Dignity model, structure, and techniques honor us.

Yet much has changed since that first publication. Who could have guessed that so many students would be victimized by violence and bullying, some rationally fearing for their lives? How many would have predicted that the airwaves would be filled with hate-mongering language and musical lyrics that make hardened inner-city students sound like choirboys? Was there any way to have known that students could photograph their tests and send them in a nanosecond to their friends on cell phones or that the buzz and distraction of students texting each other would be a common fixture in every school? It is equally doubtful that most teachers would have thought that nearly every class would be filled with a group of students of wide-ranging intellectual, cultural, and emotional diversity. Now part of the fabric of education, inclusion is here to stay.

A year after the second edition of *Discipline with Dignity* (Curwin & Mendler, 1999a), the word *Columbine* became a household name. Incidents like the shooting at that Colorado school changed the way we understood school safety and increased the responsibility to both protect and connect with all students. Because of Columbine and other school shootings, district and school policies were created much out of fear and desperation. "Zero tolerance" became the catchword against certain acts deemed inappropriate. While the idea (safety) behind zero tolerance was primarily good, many of these policies have limited the effectiveness of teachers and administrators. Although policies can provide guidance, when zero tolerance is used to expel a kindergarten student for having an aspirin bottle, all must agree that the policy has gone too far. Many educators are frustrated by the number of policies they are required to follow on a daily basis.

Discipline with Dignity is predicated on the fact that one size does not fit all. Teachers need flexibility to use their judgment. We suggest a program in which being fair does not mean having to treat everyone exactly the same way. Do we want our students to have "zero tolerance" for each other when in an argument on the playground, on the bus, or in the lunchroom?

Envision is a charter school project consisting of four schools in the Bay Area that serve primarily low-income urban youth. Its practices represent much of what we recommend in this book. Envision emphasizes community building, real learning, high expectations, and treating everyone with dignity. A major incident occurred the day before we made our visit to one of the schools, the Impact Academy in Hayward, California, that illustrates how our understanding of children's lives has changed.

On that morning, two gunmen stole a car and were attempting armed robberies near the school. While in pursuit of the gunmen, the police mistook a 14-year-old student of the school for one of them. Dwayne, a charming, warm, and easygoing young man, was shoved to the ground and handcuffed. Six police officers aimed their weapons at him and demanded that he not move. Jen Davis Wickens, the superb school principal, saw this incident and ran out to tell the police that they had the wrong person, but the officers held Dwayne on the ground for about another half hour before releasing him. One might expect Dwayne to have been upset and angry, but instead he said, "I'm not mad. This happens in my neighborhood all the time." Although we are grateful for the diligence of the police in making a split-second decision that might have prevented an armed criminal from getting loose in the school, the possibility of racial profiling and the officers' refusal to immediately release Dwayne are very bothersome.

In a community meeting, Jen Davis Wickens asked how many other students had experienced being wrongly accused. Far too many indicated an affirmative answer. For most educators, this is hard to imagine. Few of us have ever been wrongly accused of a crime or had six guns pointed at our heads. After an incident like this, is it even possible to get back to teaching and learning math and science?

So many nonschool factors affect student behavior, yet the challenge we face as educators is to maximize the power we do have to influence the lives of children. Many children once labeled "at risk" who grow up to be successful often attribute their success to a caring teacher who took a special interest in them. There is much that competes for the hearts, minds, and souls of our students. When we fail to capture their interest, vulnerability to drugs, gangs, and other unsavory influences increases. Schools must find ways to successfully compete with gangs to meet the needs of children.

Discipline with Dignity offers an affirming approach to discipline that promotes respect for self and others. It emphasizes specific strategies and structures for educators to help all students, including the "throwaways," be successful.

To make the rewrite of this book as relevant and useful as we could, we thoroughly examined each chapter, paying careful attention to four factors:

- Given the changes in the world, society, school, and students themselves, what in the chapter is less relevant or perhaps not relevant at all?
- Given the same changes, what needs to be added to help with new problems and student behaviors?
- What should we keep that still has strong merit with updated, real-life examples?
- Could we continue to affirm all of the principles, beliefs, and values at the core of this approach? Did some need to be eliminated with new ones added or others changed to accommodate the realities of today?

At the beginning of each chapter, we have added a section called "What We Have Learned." In this section we review what has changed in schools and the ways students behave that address the concerns just listed. We then added to, subtracted from, or reinforced the previously written chapter to make its material relevant in today's classrooms. Much was significantly redesigned, some only slightly. What follows is a book true to our original vision and our beliefs that is, in our view, up-to-date and current, without losing what made *Discipline with Dignity* so special in earlier editions.

We enjoyed writing this edition and learned much from the process. More important, we believe that our efforts will help improve the lives of children. Nothing is better than that.

1

Discipline

In this overview chapter on discipline, originally written 20 years ago, we explore both out-of-school and in-school causes of discipline problems. Sadly, the out-of-school causes that we originally wrote about have only worsened, and new ones have emerged. In 1988, the year of first publication, there had been no Columbine or Virginia Tech shootings. The staggering 18,000 acts of television violence witnessed by children as they entered adolescence have since grown to hundreds of thousands. The frequent "subliminal" messages of sex and violence purveyed through print and electronic media are now so overt that our airwaves are filled with violent and sexually exploitative television shows, movies, words, actions, titles, and video games. Although *Father Knows Best* was a thing of the past even in 1988, we were still a long way from Fox's *Who's Your Daddy?* There was no Internet back then offering chat rooms filled with whatever you want, whenever you want it, or blogs from people spouting any crazy message.

For all the legal advances we have made in gender, racial, and sexual preference equality, the problems of bullying are at least as bad as they have always been and have even taken new forms, such as cyberbullying. Segregation, while illegal for many years now in the United States, seems more the norm than the exception when it comes to schooling. Although we have known for many years of the correlation between socioeconomic status (SES) and achievement, white flight to the suburbs has left urban America with a preponderance of schools with a very high concentration of poverty and therefore arguably a school culture less likely to reinforce high achievement. Despite employing early intervention, monitoring academic progress, differentiating instruction, adding career-themed curricula, reconfiguring middle and high schools to create smaller classes, and emphasizing high standards with high-stakes tests, graduation rates in urban areas remain abysmal. For example, New York State Department of Education statistics show that 45 percent of high school students in the "big four" cities of upstate New York graduate four years after starting high school versus about 85 percent in the suburbs (Loudon & McLendon, 2007).

The "me generation" we talked about in the first edition has grown into a world where many expect entitlement without effort. The continued erosion of social civility, often poorly modeled by our political, civic, and entertainment leaders, has legitimized name-calling, blame, and meanness as acceptable methods by which to express disagreement. These troublesome activities are often experienced in the home by our most difficult students.

Our observations and experiences tell us that somewhere between 70 and 90 percent of discipline problems have their root causes in places outside school—the aforementioned issues as well as others, including dysfunctional families and drug and alcohol abuse. Although educators can directly do little to change these factors, it is important that we understand them and do whatever we can as citizens to make a difference. More important is to appreciate that the 10 to 30 percent of the factors we do control, which are wrapped inside the in-school causes, can change many lives when we maximize the impact of positively affecting these factors (Marzano, 2003). An hour a day helping students to be cared about, listened to, and thought of as productive, useful members of class is better than none at all.

This chapter explores both in-school and out-of-school causes of discipline problems. It shares suggestions about each and concludes with an overview of our approach to discipline. Although social and educational changes have undoubtedly occurred since this book's first publication, the framework offered in *Discipline with Dignity* remains as relevant today as ever.

In 1907, William Chandler Bagley of the University of Illinois wrote:

> Absolute fearlessness is the first essential for the teacher on whom rests the responsibility for governing an elementary or secondary school. This fearlessness is not alone or chiefly the expression of physical courage, although this must not be lacking. It is rather an expression of moral courage; daring the sometimes certain interference of parents, officious trustees [administrators] and others of like character; standing firm in one's convictions even though the community may not approve. And, after all, it is this sort of courage that is the rarest and, at the same time, the most essential. (p. 105)

In 2006, Michael Carey, a high school senior from Rochester, New York, wrote the following poem about his experiences in school:

School, if that's what you call it . . .
Even when I'm here, I'm never all there
Your work is so hard; I'm pulling my hair
My friends all do well, but I can't compare
I work really hard, but As are so rare
You yell and scream right into my face
Your not a teacher, you're a fu**ing disgrace
Not just to me but to other students too
We all hate school; the one we hate most is you
The work is so hard, the math is so tough
This school would be fun, if it wasn't so rough
Children fight each other to prove they're not weak
They fight each other, our futures so bleak.
I wish I was happy, I wish school was great
I'm 16 years old and you said "it's too late!"
For me to change and learn how to read
Why do I come? I'll never succeed
I try my best; it's not good enough
Why do I bother so I leave in a huff!

For at least the 10 decades between the writings of Dr. Bagley and Michael, teachers and students have often needed courage to face each other. School is a battleground for too many participants, a place where major confrontations and minor skirmishes occur daily. Why must this be so? Teachers and students share the same space, time, goals, and needs. They spend most of the day communicating with each other, thinking about each other, scheming against each other, and judging each other. When they are antagonistic, they expend as much if not more time and energy trying to outsmart each other and win, or at least achieve a standoff. If things get bad enough, they have the power to ruin each other's lives. When things go well, they share tender moments, meaningful triumphs, and genuine respect and love. Regardless of how their relationship goes, teachers and students never forget each other.

Much has been written about discipline over the years, and many programs and methods have been tried and retried with new names. The issue will always be an integral part of school because students will always learn more than the content of the curriculum. They will learn about their behavior, their choices, and their impact on others. Instead of trying to solve the discipline problem, it might be wiser to try to positively affect the lives of children. We strongly advocate and propose a model of discipline based on a positive value system and suggest many practical methods to implement such a system in the classroom. Good discipline is about doing what is best for students to make good, healthy choices, not about making the lives of educators easier. A wise educator once suggested that if you always do what's in the best interest of children, there will always be a place for you in education, and you will always make some people angry!

This book describes strategies for developing a philosophy about behavior and classroom management based on sound educational, psychological, and commonsense principles. This will include

• Developing a comprehensive classroom discipline plan,
• Preventing behavior and management problems from occurring,
• Stopping misbehavior when it occurs without attacking the dignity of the student,
• Resolving problems with students who chronically disrupt the learning process,
• Reducing student stress as well as your own, and
• Using special guidelines for rules and consequences that work.

Out-of-School Causes of Discipline Problems

Jon, a student growing up in foster care, summed it up:

> I do not even have parents. I mean, not a mom and a dad the way you would think of it. You see, I live in a foster home, which means I go home every single night to paid employees. Most of the people that work at the place have their own children. They do not really care about me. Sure, they are supposed to . . . but just like any other job, many are here to pick up a paycheck or wait for their next vacation. They act happy when I get a good grade, or have a good report card, but it's nothing like most children get to experience when they get home! Holidays and breaks are a disaster for me. I do not ever get to go on vacation like most of the other children here. Instead, I get to sit home thinking about where my real mom is, why she left me, and if I'll ever see her again. Honestly, your English homework is the farthest thing from my mind right now.

Sadly, this student is not alone, and success for children like him is rare. According to Christian (2003), the educational deficits of foster children are reflected in higher rates of grade retention; lower scores on standardized tests; and higher absenteeism, tardiness, truancy, and dropout rates. The poor academic performance of these children affects their lives after foster care and contributes to higher-than-average rates of homelessness, criminality, drug abuse, and unemployment among foster care "graduates."

We do not mean to imply that discipline problems in school are the responsibility of the foster care system. Some children go home to dysfunctional biological families. In these homes many of the basics are not taught. Words like *please*, *thank you*, and *share* are not used, so children never learn the appropriate way to use them. In some families, the values necessary for success at school are either untaught or, more important, unlived. Good discipline is increasingly about educators taking the time to teach parenting-type skills, so students will have the self-control to learn the basics and beyond.

Much of this book addresses what can be done about discipline problems, but it is first necessary to consider those factors responsible for the alienation experienced by too many youths in schools. The causes of discipline problems are discussed because it is our belief that discipline prevention and successful intervention hinge on an understanding of both in-school and out-of-school issues that strongly influence student behavior. Just as good medicine often depends on knowing the specifics, so, too, does good teaching. For example, imagine two people with really bad headaches. A physician determines that the first patient's headache is caused by eyestrain. She gets glasses, and the headache goes away. The second patient learns he has a brain tumor and will need immediate surgery. In this example both patients have the same symptom, but without understanding why the headache exists, each cannot be properly treated.

In figuring out why a disruption happens, it is sometimes wise to ask the student. To get a valid answer, we must press beyond students saying, "I don't know" and "He did it first." In a calmer moment, it is appropriate to say, "I do not like being called a fu**ing a**hole and talking to me in that way is entirely unacceptable. You are better than that! Before we look at an appropriate consequence, what happened to make you so angry?" When a student does something inappropriate, it is important to teach a better way to respond, model the behavior we want the student to exhibit, and maintain everyone's dignity.

Without our belaboring the social ills of our world, the fact is that we live in a society where resolving problems through shootings, knifings, fist fights, extortion, bullying, and threats of injury are commonplace. Children are constantly exposed to violence, and many have become insensitive to it. The backdrop of war has been a theme for the entirety of entering kindergartners' lives. Loss of American soldiers while fighting the war on terror is so common that their deaths rarely make front-page news anymore. In addition, children do what is done to them. If parents hit, yell, or humiliate their child on a regular basis, we can expect the same behavior from the child.

Effects of the Media

Although it is impossible to know the full extent of the influence of standard programming, we believe that television and other media have a potentially damaging effect on children. A recent study that reviewed a decade of research concerning television and youth concluded that children will have viewed 200,000 acts of violence—including16,000 murders—by the time they are 18 years of age (Media Education Foundation, 2005). According to another study (Curwin, 2006), 75 percent of 4th graders claimed to have watched an R-rated movie, 65 percent said they had played a violent video game, and 84 percent said they had witnessed at least one killing on television in the prior year.

A Sense of Entitlement

A sense of entitlement has gripped our culture. An informal study in *Newsweek* (Tyre, Scelfo, & Kantrowitz, 2004) found that children expect to nag their parents nine times before getting what they want. The net result is that too many students have a "me first" attitude: "Meet my needs first. I do not intend to wait. I come first." Unwittingly, many schools reinforce this sense of entitlement through the proliferation of reward and bribe systems in which stickers, stars, and points become substitutes for doing the right thing because it is the right thing to do.

With just the push of a button, we can communicate with anyone anywhere in the world. We can download thousands of songs in seconds on our iPods, be entertained nonstop by DVDs that we start and stop at our command, and enter a virtual world doing almost anything instantly with amazing graphics. When students realize that As and Bs at school aren't just given but must be earned and that timely thought and study is at least sometimes required to master a concept, some become frustrated and angry at the audacity of an "unfair" teacher trying to hold them accountable in a world for which they have been poorly prepared.

Lack of a Secure Family Environment

Perhaps the largest single influence on children is the quality of their home life. Throughout the last century, our society has undergone major shifts in values and traditions. The extended family has been replaced by smaller nuclear units in a multitude of configurations. Single-parent families, two-working-parent families, two-mommy or -daddy parents, blended families, and one- and two-child families are likely to exist in just about every community. Amid constantly shifting family patterns, a discipline problem is often symptomatic of anxiety and insecurity.

The U.S. divorce rate has steadily risen so that some states have more divorces than marriages. It is not a secret that children of divorced parents perform worse than their peers in most academic settings (Crow & Ward-Lonergan, 2003). Although divorce is not necessarily a predictor of problems at school, children with divorced parents are more likely to be struggling with issues of emotional security than their classmates from more stable families. In 1970, 12 percent of children were born to unwed parents, compared with almost 35 percent more recently (Sigle-Rushton & McLanahan, 2002). Data from the National

Center for Health Statistics found that in 2004, more than 1.5 million babies were born to unwed mothers. Although the birthrate for teenagers 15 to 19 years old showed a recent modest decline of 2 percent in 2005 (Hamilton, Martin, & Ventura, 2006), it is still far too high.

Students are coming to school more concerned for their basic security needs than for learning. These security issues have created a large group of needy children seeking emotional support from just about anybody available.

Diminished Social Civility

When our political and civic leaders cannot discuss issues without pointing the finger of blame, calling each other names, and painting their opponent as evil, is it any wonder that children see name-calling and put-downs as acceptable methods of communication? When song lyrics sometimes include offensive language and use of hateful and unacceptable words like *nigger, faggot, wetback, Jew-down*, and *ho* is considered OK as long as you belong to a certain ethnic group, the boundaries of civility and decency have been ruptured. Good discipline is far more difficult when these boundaries are hard to identify.

Concentration of Poverty

Numerous studies over many years have shown a strong correlation between socioeconomic status and success in school. Generally speaking, students from wealthier families do significantly better than those from poorer families. In nearly every community across America, parents seek the best schools for their children. Although there are exceptions, the schools with the best reputations are almost always in upper-middle-class suburbia with a preponderance of white children. Although these schools are typically blessed with greater resources, just as many boring teachers work at these schools as at others. Could it be that these schools have a cultural expectation of success bred by the vast majority of students who are from homes that strongly value the importance of educational achievement? Isn't it probable that the majority of students in these schools have parents who are themselves more likely to be highly educated and therefore successful in our culture? If lower-SES students tend to achieve more poorly than their wealthier peers, isn't it likely that when you put lots of these children together at the same school, a culture that does not value high achievement is more likely to emerge?

The "best schools" have a culture among their students where it is cool to be successful in school. In too many poorly performing schools, achievement is considered to be uncool or a sign of selling out. Top students often feel like they need to hide being smart.

On a recent visit with 11-year-old Victor, one of the authors' "little brothers" in the Big Brothers Big Sisters program, Victor spontaneously said that he would never want to go away to college because he wouldn't want to leave his family. When this very bright boy was asked if he knew anyone in his neighborhood who was going to college, Victor could not think of a single person. Sadly, he is one of many who face an uphill struggle to success because he has no community context for how education can really improve life. A recent discussion with one of the authors' friends makes a similar point. The friend, who lives in a small enclave of beautifully maintained homes within an otherwise decaying city, matter-of-factly noted that all the young families move out as soon as their children reach school age because they do not want to send their children to an urban school.

In a gang-infested middle school in San Jose, one of the authors interviewed several students who, when asked about their plans for the future, said, "Go to prison." When asked why, they responded, "That's how you get respect around here."

Radical solutions to this problem may be necessary. Perhaps the time has come to use socioeconomic status (or perhaps even race) to define school enrollment. We would like to see how students perform in schools where no more that 20 percent of its students are on free and reduced lunch. Our speculation is that all schools should have approximately 10 to 20 percent of its population be of lower-SES status but no more. We believe that no school should open when its low-SES students exceed 20 percent unless geographically impossible. Exceptions would be in some rural areas in which great distances might make economic diversity unrealistic. Although problems are likely to arise that would need to be addressed, we would hypothesize sufficient diversity within such schools amid a culture that values school success.

Although there are few quick-fix solutions to the factors cited here, an impressive base of research strongly suggests that a caring, mentoring relationship often plays a huge role in contributing to the resiliency of at-risk youth (Ellis, Small-McGinley, & De Fabrizio, 1999; Werner & Smith, 1989). Educators get daily opportunities to offer students this type of nurturance that can dramatically impact student behavior and sometimes change lives.

In-School Causes of Discipline Problems and Some Solutions

Competitive Environment

Most schools remain highly competitive environments where students compete for recognition, grades, and spots on sports teams. It is important to realize that academic competition is very different from real-life competition. In life, people get a chance to compete in a field, profession, or industry of their own choice. If unsuccessful, they can switch to a different career or profession. By contrast, in school we drop all 7-year-olds in 2nd grade and say, "Go at it." When some do not succeed, we begin labeling them as problem students. Competition is fine when playing on the football field or basketball court and when trying out for the school musical. When limited roles exist, competition is necessary to get the best people for the job. Competition between people is fine when children know there is a chance they will not make the team or the show, but they want to try anyway.

With regard to academic achievement and behavioral improvement, replace the concept of competition *between* students with competition *within* each student. Whenever possible, evaluate student performance and offer assignments based on getting each student to be better today than he was yesterday. An individual's improvement is primarily what should be acknowledged. Conversely, if a student shows lesser performance than her capability, she should be challenged to do better even if her initial performance is best in the class.

One of the authors recently asked his 17-year-old sister if she had made honor roll. Looking surprised, she said, "What's honor roll?" When told it was a list you make when you get really good grades for a semester, her response was "At Brighton High School [a top 100 high school in America located in a suburb of Rochester, New York], everyone is expected to get good grades. We do not get on a list for that. And besides, why would I want to be on a list for doing well? It would just make my friends who didn't get on the list feel bad!" Although honor rolls are institutional fixtures at most schools, we believe their elimination would make schools better places. How about replacing competition between students for an "honor roll" spot with daily recognition for all students who are "on a roll"?

Student Boredom

Some students sit up straight, appear attentive by making eye contact, nod their heads every so often, and present themselves as interested and somewhat involved, even when they are downright bored. But there are others who show no desire to hide their boredom. They quietly withdraw into themselves and look unmotivated, or they act out, being unconcerned with the consequences of poor grades, a trip to the principal's office, a mark on the chalkboard, or a phone call home.

Powerlessness

Powerlessness is another factor in school and classroom discipline problems. Some students rebel as a way of voicing their dissatisfaction with their lack of influence. In most schools, students are told for six hours every day where to go, what time to be there, how long to take for basic biological necessities, which learning is relevant, what to learn, and how their learning will be evaluated. They are told the rules, the consequences, how to dress, how to walk, and when to talk. When one group (adults) develops rules and procedures that define behavioral standards for another group (students) that has had little or no input, a conflict of control and power can result. When school is unfulfilling, this lack of power can trigger anger and opposition.

Unclear Limits

Limit setting is very important to good discipline and improved behavior. Teachers and administrators need to be very clear and specific as to the behaviors they will and will not tolerate. In addition, we promote respect for and among our students when we explain why the limits are as they are. Although many educators intuitively know this, our busy lives too often preclude spending adequate time to address this issue.

Requiring Students to Earn Educational Opportunities

Most schools require that education opportunities be earned instead of given. These opportunities include field trips, pizza parties, playground privileges, and even staying in the classroom. The students who need these opportunities the most are the ones who rarely earn them. Because they feel left out, students tend to denigrate the opportunities denied them by calling the activities "stupid," or worse. The good students get increased opportunities to learn social skills and to feel wanted, while the poor students rarely get the experience needed to improve behavior. Most just feel left out.

Lack of Acceptable Outlets to Express Feelings

Another source of discipline problems is the lack of acceptable outlets for expressing feelings (for both students and teachers). Students and teachers need to have acceptable ways to release emotions, thoughts, and feelings.

Attacks on Dignity

Finally, and most significant, many students with chronic behavior problems believe that they cannot and will not be successful in school. Such students often appear to give up before they have even tried. They do not believe they can receive the attention and recognition they need through school achievement. They see themselves as losers and have ceased trying to gain acceptance in the mainstream. Their self-message is "Since I can't be recognized as anything other than a failure, I'll protect myself from feeling hurt. To do nothing is better than to try and fail. And to be recognized as a troublemaker is better than being seen as stupid."

Schools Do Make a Difference: Discipline with Dignity

Discipline problems have existed for as long as schools. Any time a group of 25 to 30 people are in close proximity to each other for six hours every day, 10 months of the year, a variety of interpersonal conflicts occur. Discipline with Dignity offers a three-pronged approach to taking charge of such conflict.

- **Prevention**—what can be done to prevent problems from occurring?
- **Action**—what can be done when misbehavior occurs to solve the problem without making it worse?
- **Resolution**—what can be done for students who are chronically challenging?

Foundation of the Program

If we allow ourselves to become helpless in the face of the many causes of misbehavior, it becomes very difficult to teach. Discipline with Dignity is designed to help the teacher work effectively with children despite these numerous problems. The 12-step plan that follows is a guide for teachers. Each step represents specific things educators can do to ensure the success of their students, help prevent discipline problems, and intervene when disruption does occur.

1. Let students know what you need, and ask them what they need from you. Most teachers only do the first part. It is easy for us to tell them what we need. However, the best teachers also ask students what they need.

2. Differentiate instruction based on each student's strengths. If a student is acting out, assume that this is his defense against feeling like a failure because he cannot, or believes he cannot, handle the material. If you are unable or unwilling to adapt your teaching style to lower or higher academic levels based on the student's needs, then you should not be surprised when that student is disruptive.

Just as expectations that are too high lead to frustration, those that are too low lead to boredom and the feeling that success is cheap and not worthy of effort. When we make learning too easy, students find little value in it and little pride in their achievements. It is important to increase the challenge without increasing the tedium.

3. Listen to what students are thinking and feeling. There is probably no skill more important than active listening to defuse potentially troublesome situations. For example, Denise says, "Mrs. Lewis, this lesson is soooo boring. I hate it." A "button-pushed" response would be "Well, maybe if you paid more attention and did some work once in a while, you'd feel differently." A better response that defuses might be "I hear you, and I'm sorry you feel that way. Why not give me a suggestion or two that will help make it better? Please see me right after class."

4. Use humor. We are not paid to be comedians, nor should we be expected to come to class prepared with an arsenal of jokes. But many frustrating situations can be lightened by learning how to poke fun at ourselves and by avoiding defensiveness.

Make sure students are not the butt of your jokes. Bill, a 7th grade student obviously intent on hooking Ms. Johnson into a power struggle, announced one day in class as he looked squarely at his teacher, "You are a mother fu**er!" Ms. Johnson responded by looking at the student and saying, "Wow, at least you got it half right!" The class laughed, and a tense moment had abated. It is important to note that it is almost always better to give a consequence or otherwise more fully explore what to do about highly inappropriate behavior at a time that does not take away further from classroom instruction. We explore this issue in more depth in Chapters 6 and 8.

5. Vary your style of presentation. Older children have a maximum attention span of 15 minutes and younger children 10 minutes for any one style of presentation. If we lecture for 15 minutes, it helps to have a discussion for the next interval. If we have a large-group discussion, switch to small groups. Continually using the same approach will create inattentiveness and restlessness, which may lead to disruption.

6. Offer choices. Teachers and administrators need to constantly be looking for places during the school day to allow children to make decisions. For example: "You can do your assignment now or during recess." "You can borrow a pencil or buy one from me." "When people call you names you can tell them you don't like it, walk away, or ask me for a suggestion." Allowing students to make decisions and then live with the outcome of the decision goes a long way in teaching responsibility.

7. Refuse to accept excuses, and stop making them yourself. When students are allowed to explain away their misbehavior, you place yourself in the uncomfortable position of being judge and jury. Students with good excuses learn that a good excuse will avoid trouble. Students with bad excuses learn that they need some practice in improving their excuse making. Either way, accepting excuses teaches students how to be irresponsible. If you consider certain excuses legitimate, try to include them as part of the rules so they are clearly stated before an incident occurs. It can be helpful to provide students with an explanation as to why certain excuses are considered legitimate while others are not.

Teachers should hold themselves accountable, too. For example, if the rule is that all students will turn in their homework within 24 hours, promise your students feedback within 24 hours or an automatic *A* if you are late. Holding ourselves accountable keeps us from making the same kinds of excuses we hate hearing from our students.

8. Legitimize misbehavior that you cannot stop. If you have done everything possible to stop a certain behavior and it continues, think of creative ways to legitimize it. If there are daily paper airplane flights buzzing past your ear, consider spending five minutes a day having paper airplane contests. If abusive language persists, ask the student to publicly define the offensive words to ensure understanding. If your students like to complain about one thing or another, have a gripe session or a suggestion box in which students are encouraged to deposit their complaints. If your school has chronic disruptions in study hall, then offer a game-filled, nonacademic study hall in addition to one that is quiet for those who really want to study. When misbehavior is legitimized within boundaries, the fun of acting out often fizzles.

9. Use a variety of ways to communicate with children. In addition to the spoken word, caring gestures and nonverbal messages can be effective. Some students do better when they get feedback on a sticky note, in an e-mailed note, or on a cell phone message. Since the original publication of this book, there have been numerous reports of inappropriate relationships between teachers and students. Although touch can be a very effective way to communicate caring, we understand that many educators have become wary. Certainly, we need to be respectful of physical boundaries, and we must never touch a student when seduction or abuse is even a remote possibility. Although there is no substitute for good judgment, a pat on the back, touch on the shoulder, handshake, or high five can help form bonds with many tough-to-reach children.

10. Be responsible for yourself, and allow children to take responsibility for themselves. Teachers are responsible for coming to class on time, presenting their subject in as interesting a fashion as they can, returning papers with meaningful comments in a reasonable period of time, providing help for students having difficulty, and ending class on time. Students are responsible for bringing their books, pencils, and completed homework.

11. Realize that you will not reach every child, but act as if you can. Some students, after all is said and done, must be allowed to choose failure. However, there is a difference between reality (we won't reach everyone) and belief (we work each day as if today will be the breakthrough). It is important that we access and sustain optimism so that we can continually persist in making it difficult for our students to fail our class or themselves.

12. Start fresh every day. What happened yesterday is finished. Today is a new day. Act accordingly. Stop listening to negativity from other faculty members. Instead, make a point to have a positive attitude every time you step foot in the school building.

For the Administrator

The Safe School Study (U.S. Department of Health, Education, and Welfare, 1978), followed by more recent research (Postlethwaite & Ross, 1992; Rosen 2005), clearly indicates that administrators are extremely important in reducing discipline problems and maintaining a safe school. In these schools, many principals provided extra academic work for outstanding students and encouraged students to challenge themselves. Administrators made special attempts to get children to take Advanced Placement classes. One principal even made himself available one hour per day as a tutor. Students were able to sign up for 15-minute blocks of time where he would work with them on academic concerns. Strong educational leadership had principals setting goals, evaluating performance, monitoring teachers and students, and modeling appropriate ways to behave and act (Blase & Kirby, 2000).

We suggest that the first step the administrator can take to improve discipline at school is to set up an atmosphere that encourages faculty members to discuss problems freely and openly, without fear of censure. Teachers often worry that they will be considered weak or incompetent if they admit to problems with student behavior. When we do staff development training, we usually ask the teachers who have discipline problems to raise their hands. Only one or two hands go up. But when we ask, "How many of you know another teacher in the school who has discipline problems?" every hand is raised. Once an open atmosphere exists, positive things can begin to happen. Also, it is important to encourage less experienced teachers to speak up. There is an unwritten code in most schools that says, "The more experience the better." This statement is partially true. But we have found that veteran teachers and administrators can learn as much, if not more, from less experienced educators.

We find that most school faculties represent a wide range of feelings, beliefs, and attitudes when it comes to discipline. Some teachers support having many rules, strictly enforced, with the administration being tough in every case with student violators. Other teachers feel that it is best to have few rules, with an emphasis on students solving their own problems. Effective school discipline requires a common vision predicated on what is best for students. We need to challenge our teachers and encourage them to challenge each other to clearly articulate how their beliefs and practices are in our students' best interests.

To help focus discussion, begin with the list of in-school causes of misbehavior described earlier. Set up working groups or task forces on each of the following causes: competitive environments, student boredom, powerlessness, unclear limits, lack of acceptable outlets for expressing feelings, and attacks on dignity. Each group should include teachers, administrators, parents, and students (both high- and low-achieving). Then have them develop a specific plan for your school to address each area. You will get differing opinions and thoughts. Arguments will occasionally erupt. But remember, if we always do what's best for children, the decision will become clearer.

A group in a suburban middle school tackled the issue of giving students a greater sense of control over what happens in their school by involving them in the following ways:

• A student council of "poor achievers" and "in-trouble students" (different labels were used) was created to help set school policy and to help modify rules and consequences.

• Students who served detention were given the job of commenting on how school climate could be improved.

• Students took the job of running the school for a day once a year, with the teachers and administrators taking student roles.

• Each class was required to have at least two student rules for the teacher.

Committees such as the ones suggested here are most beneficial when they are expected to develop a specific plan for action. The plan should state what will be done, who will do it, when it will be done, and how it will be evaluated. Each member of the school community (teachers, parents, administrators, students, librarians, nurses, bus drivers, and other staff) should know clearly and specifically what his or her responsibilities will be for the success of the plan. Strive for at least 75 percent agreement on any aspect of the plan before it is implemented unless the committee was given authority to develop binding recommendations.

Finally, encourage your staff members to use the practice scenarios in Appendix A as a way of generating meaningful discussion as well as providing staff with practical ways of handling challenging situations.

2

Dignity and Responsibility in the Classroom

❧ WHAT WE HAVE LEARNED ❧

Nearly everyone now agrees that for students to learn responsibility, they must be taught and encouraged to make decisions. Yet the increased pressure of testing and standards has given teachers even less time and energy for effectively helping students make improved decisions.

It is ironic that in the first edition of this chapter we wrote, "We would all be horrified if we were asked to teach all students the same content in the same way at the same speed." Yet newer concepts like curriculum alignment and curriculum mapping that have become widely accepted and promoted by educational leaders create these very conditions. Although curriculum mapping can help some teachers organize their school year, some states and districts have taken the concept way too far. Increasingly, teachers are given scripts that they have to follow day in and day out. Under this type of system, it is difficult to use elements such as creativity, relationship building, and spontaneity to create lessons that engage students.

We have further learned that most behavioral instruction comes more from informal interaction with students built on good relationships than from enforcing rules. Like good homes, classrooms are living places where needs and feelings can be expressed without resorting to formality and force. Because we define rules as what we will enforce, they should be saved for only what matters most. We have learned over the years that rules provide little motivation for students to follow them. It is the values on which the rules are based that provide the motivation. When students know the reasons for rules, they are more willing to honor them and more likely to accept the consequences for breaking them.

Core Beliefs for Effective Discipline

Managing student behavior is a complex task. There is a delicate balance between meeting the needs of the group by maintaining social order and meeting the unique needs of each student. Few choices work for all teachers and all students. We believe that the best decisions for managing student behavior are based on a value system that maintains the dignity of each student in all situations. Behaving responsibly is more valued than behaving obediently. Encouraging responsible behavior requires valuing what students think, seeking their input, and teaching them how to make good decisions. We know behavior change is slow, occurring in small increments. Expecting that students will change long-standing maladaptive behavior on demand causes more problems than it solves. We advocate a discipline model that is highly structured yet flexible at the same time—rather like a parent who sets clear, firm limits ("You can watch one hour of television per night") but offers choices within those limits ("So would you prefer 6 to 7, 7 to 8, or 8 to 9?"). We try to avoid the gimmicky, trendy, and simplistic approaches that stop misbehavior but also reduce the student's desire and love of learning.

Discipline with Dignity is based on fundamental core beliefs that are central to all effective behavior-based programs. They define the parameters of a healthy classroom that uses discipline as a learning process rather than a system of retribution. These core beliefs are as follows:

• **Dealing with student behavior is part of the job.** We have already pointed out that teaching is more positive when managing student behavior is perceived as part of the job. After all, no matter how much you love teaching the story of Macbeth, the causes of the Civil War, or how to factor binomial equations, the lessons students learn about behavior, communication, and getting along with others make a more lasting impression.

• **Always treat students with dignity.** In school, we must let students know that their dignity will always be maintained. There is no better way to damage students' dignity than to embarrass them in front of their friends, scold them in public, or have them fail in front of the class. Dignity is enhanced when students have opportunities to lead, make decisions, and give input. It becomes part of the school's fabric when they are viewed as partners in creating and sustaining the school climate, rather than simply being recipients of adult efforts.

• **Discipline works best when integrated with effective teaching practices.** We previously mentioned critical thinking as an example of using content in discipline. The processes of planning, making choices, evaluating, and analyzing results are all components of a critical thinking system. These same processes can be used as consequences when a child breaks a rule. In this system, students live what they learn, giving real-life experience to both behavior and the mastery of content. Chapter 9 examines the relationship between behavior and the practice of teaching in great detail. When we realize the importance of the relationship between good teaching and good discipline, we can prevent many problems and excite children about learning.

• **Adults see it as their professional responsibility to make positive, consistent connections with students.** Educators do not have the luxury to choose which students to support and which to ignore. We believe it is relatively easy to teach well-behaved, intrinsically motivated students. Furthermore, it is easy to like and therefore choose to engage "good" students. By contrast, difficult students say and do things that can be offensive and obnoxious. They often try to get adults angry with the goal of proving that nobody can be trusted. It is these very students who need their teachers to be tougher at not giving up on them than they are in pushing our buttons. Although it can be difficult, good discipline flourishes when adults consistently reach out to their more challenging students. We must have the skills and desire to form supportive relationships with all of our students.

• **Acting out is sometimes an act of sanity.** When children act out, they provide feedback to the teacher. The teacher misses the opportunity to improve if he punishes misbehavior without examining how he might have contributed to it. When children misbehave because of poor teaching, it is better for all if the teacher can use that information to improve his skills rather than to hide problems.

• **Fair is not always equal**. Most teachers believe that instruction must be matched to the ability and talent of each student. Differentiated instruction (Tomlinson, 2005) is predicated on such practice. No thoughtful, well-intentioned educator would ever propose it best *to teach all students the same content in the same way at the same speed.* Thomas Jefferson, one of the founding fathers of the United States, believed that it was unfair to treat unequals equally. Even our government does not advocate single solutions to all problems. Judges want and need the discretionary powers of their office to enforce the best possible sentence for a particular crime.

Teachers need the same authority when it comes to discipline. Any plan that imposes a system at the cost of teacher judgment is demeaning and ill spirited. It takes decision making away and often forces educators to do things that they know will be ineffective because the plan says so. The plan that is presented in this book is highly structured yet provides the flexibility for teacher judgment. We believe every classroom should have the principle "I will do my best to be fair, which means I will not worry about treating everyone the same way." We must do our best to give each student what he or she needs without comparing each action for one student with a different action for another. In actual practice, although we may use the same teaching method for most students, we'll need others in our toolbox for a few, and we may need to create a new one for a particularly unique learner. This concept gives us the ability and structure to work with each student at his or her level without being influenced by what the others think. More will be discussed on this very important concept in Chapter 5.

The 70-20-10 Principle

The percentages may vary from classroom to classroom, but generally speaking, a typical classroom has three groups of students. Since the first publication of this book, we believe the numbers have changed from 80-15-5 percent to 70-20-10 percent.

• **70 percent: These students rarely break rules or violate principles.** They come to school motivated to learn, prepared to work, and accepting the limits of a classroom setting. By and large, these students have been sufficiently successful by both formal and informal standards so that they expect success in the future. Most discipline plans are either unnecessary or intrusive to these students, although they can provide structure and predictability.

• **20 percent: These students break rules on a somewhat regular basis.** They do not blindly accept the classroom principles, and they fight the restrictions. Their motivation ranges from completely on to completely off, depending on what happened at home that morning or how they perceive the daily classroom activities. Their achievement can range from high to low, depending on the teacher, the class, or their expectations for success. These students need a clear set of expectations, and teachers must follow through with consequences. If these students are not given enough structure, they can disrupt learning for all the other students. Children like these will usually follow rules as long as they see how the rule makes sense. However, they will be the first to argue something that they perceive as "unfair" or that in their minds makes no sense. These students are ideal for helping make rules. Invite their thoughts and opinions before settling on specific school or classroom rules. We like the idea of a school and classroom "rules committee" that can meet and discuss the value in certain rules. Invite these students to be a part of those committees. Ask their thoughts and opinions on how they would handle rule breakers if they were in charge. Then you can ask this group of students to help enforce the rules. Since they played a part in making them they can help by asking their friends to follow the rules.

- **10 percent: These students are chronic rule breakers and generally out of control most of the time.** Little seems to work for them. They have typically experienced failure in school from an early age and maintain no hope for success in the future. They believe there is no reason to behave or to learn. Most have learning or emotional problems and may come from troubled homes. Many, but not all, special needs students fit into this group, including attention deficit hyperactivity disorder (ADHD), autistic, bipolar, and defiant children. We offer strategies to help teachers cope with students causing severe behavior disruptions in the classroom (Chapters 8 and 10), but many such students need professional medical or psychiatric help.

The trick of a good discipline plan is to control the 20 percent without alienating or overly regulating the 70 percent and without backing the 10 percent into a corner. Heavily punitive plans tend to give the illusion that they are successful. However, the seeds are sown for chronically disruptive students to explode, for some of the 70 percent to lose interest in learning, and for many of the 20 percent to become sneakier at misbehaving. Teachers often feel trapped between their desire for consistency and the fear of coming down too hard on the rare rule violation of the naturally motivated student. They are also aware of the need to give chronically disruptive students hope and some space and to make school as positive an experience for them as possible.

The Discipline Basics

Every discipline program has in one form or another the following elements: rules, values or principles (the word *principles* is considered synonymous with *values*), enforcement or intervention procedures, and an implicit or explicit evaluation process. Each process also provides students with incidental or secondary learning about nurturing self-worth, handling responsibility, solving problems, controlling their lives, and affecting the consequences of their behavior. Figure 2.1 is a generic model of discipline that illustrates how most behavior management models function.

Figure 2.1
Generic Model of Discipline

Principles: What general attitude and behavioral guidelines teachers model and students are encouraged to learn in class

Rules: What is enforced every time it is broken

Enforcement or intervention: What happens when a rule is broken

Student (incidental) Learning: What the student learns as a result of the enforcement/intervention

Evaluation: How well the discipline program is working

Rules

Rules are what we are willing to enforce. They are central to all discipline programs, but they are often overemphasized. Consequences and values are more influential for achieving long-term behavior change. Rules maintain order for the present. Rules work best when they are behavioral and written in black-and-white terms. Students and teachers should easily see whether a specific behavior violates a rule. Airlines demonstrate the perfect balance between rules and values. Before every flight, the attendant typically says something like, "The number one value of this airline is safety." Then the rules are stated in exact behavioral terms, all related to safety.

- Fasten your seatbelts.
- Make sure your tray table and seatback are in the upright and locked position.
- All electronic devices must be turned off.

Notice the rules are behavioral; there is no discussion, negotiation, or cries of "We're close enough"; "Just wait, I'm right in the middle of a song"; "My father says I do not have to"; "I do not feel like it."

Here are some examples of classroom rules:

- Before speaking, raise your hand.
- Bring your books and materials to class.
- Be in your seat when the bell rings.
- Touch other students' belongings only with their permission.

When rules are vague or replaced by values (e.g., be respectful; be courteous; be kind), students have difficulty making the connection between their behavior and the consequences. *Rules* need to define *what to do and how to do it. Values* define *why we do it this way.* For example, safety and respect are values that mean many things. It is important that students know "Hands and feet must be kept to ourselves . . ." (rule), ". . . because we must respect the safety of others" (value). Rules guided by values are necessary for effective discipline.

Values or Principles

Because values cannot be enforced, they are often overlooked or ignored by packaged discipline programs. If the teacher attempts to enforce values or principles, students often blame the teacher or focus on the part of the gray area that proves them right. Can you imagine a law that demanded "Be respectful of other drivers on the road"? What behavior would result in an arrest? Although values are by definition more ambiguous and therefore require more teaching and discussion, an understanding of and exposure to sound values and principles is a crucial foundation for good rules. When rules are not developed naturally from values, students may learn a specific action without seeing or understanding its value. For example, students may learn to be in their seat when the bell rings without knowing or understanding this to be part of a larger theme: responsible work habits.

Effective discipline programs provide clear and specific rules along with guidelines for enforcement without sacrificing the higher levels of learning that principles provide.

Enforcement or Intervention Procedures

Practically speaking, consequences are more important than rules for a program to be successful, and this is why programs based on punishment and teacher power can be counterproductive. They are marketed as simple to learn, easy to implement, and quick with results, but their greatest attraction is their greatest weakness. To achieve their lofty claims, punitive programs must resort to power-based methods. They rely on an obedience model of discipline (discussed in the next section; see also Figure 2.2) because "telling students what to do" requires the least amount of work or change for the teacher. Obedience models have as their goals (1) minimal or no rule violations and (2) students following orders.

Rewards and punishments are the main intervention/enforcement procedures when seeking obedience. The results, if "successful," are fewer rule violations and, unfortunately, less student learning about responsibility. Rewards and punishments satiate. In other words, as students get used to certain rewards or punishments, these measures lose their effect. After one detention, students cry for mercy. After three detentions, they say, "Cool—I like detention. Give me a hundred. I don't care." After one level of reward, they say, "Is that all?" while wanting more. And they

---

Figure 2.2
Obedience Model of Discipline

Main goal: Students follow orders.

Principle: Do what I (the teacher or administrator) want.

Intervention: Punishment is the primary intervention.

External locus of control

Done *to* student

Examples

- Threats
- Scoldings
- Writing "I will not _____ " 500 times.
- Detentions
- Writing student's name on chalkboard

Student learns . . .

- Don't get caught.
- It's not my responsibility.

---

learn to say, "What do I get?" when asked to do anything. A good consequence needs to teach better behavior. It doesn't matter if the student feels good or bad—it matters that the student learns better behavior.

THE OBEDIENCE MODEL

We define *obedience* as following rules without question, regardless of philosophical beliefs, ideas of right and wrong, instincts and experiences, or values. A student "does it" because he is told to do it. In the short term, obedience offers teachers relief, a sense of power and control, and an oasis from the constant bombardment of defiance. In the long run, however, obedience leads to student immaturity, a lack of responsibility, an inability to think clearly and critically, and a feeling of helplessness that is manifested by withdrawal, aggressiveness, or power struggles. Obedience without responsibility, even when it "works," is not philosophically, psychologically, or sociologically defensible. However, obedience is necessary when safety is involved.

Figure 2.2 shows that the obedience model uses punishment as its main type of intervention. William Chandler Bagley knew in 1907 that punishments were to be reserved for those cases when nothing else seemed to work.

> It must be remembered that not every individual needs to be subjected to a penalty in order to ensure the inhibition of his social impulses. The infliction of a penalty is always the last resort, reserved for those cases in which all other means fail. The individual must, if necessary, be sacrificed to the mass; but the sacrifice must not be made unless the necessity is clear, nor in any greater degree than necessity demands. (p. 105)

Our view is that the highest virtue of education is to teach students to be self-responsible and fully functional. In all but extreme cases, obedience contradicts these goals. This does not mean we do not believe in consequences. We do. And children need them. But there is a huge difference between punishments and consequences. Both will be specifically addressed in Chapter 5.

Another problem common to many obedience models is the limited opportunity for teacher discretion. Some programs offer only one alternative intervention for teachers when a rule is violated. Others have a lock-step progression approach that requires a specific intervention for violation 1, another for violation 2, and so forth. Either system removes teacher judgment from the process. This cripples the teacher's ability to examine rule violations in their broader context and demeans the teacher's capacity to be a decision maker. Faced with what may be an untenable either/or choice or no choice at all, teachers often look the other way. This response is the only way they can factor in special circumstances that do not fit "the program." Over time, this approach creates numerous inconsistencies that ultimately doom the program. With such "teacherproof" programs, faculty members either subvert or redesign the system—and almost always resent using it.

THE RESPONSIBILITY MODEL

Responsibility models foster critical thinking and shared decision making. Children feel affirmed even though they do not always get their way. They understand that they have some control of the events that happen to them, and they get a chance to learn that teachers also have rights, power, knowledge, and leadership.

Teachers who subscribe to the responsibility model follow the adage "If you want true power, you must give some of it away." Students cannot learn responsibility without choices and without an opportunity to make mistakes and learn from them.

The responsibility model (Figure 2.3) is far more consistent with the current classroom emphasis on critical thinking and decision making. Consider what must students learn when the curriculum says, "Make decisions based on critical thinking skills," while they are simultaneously told, "Do what I say, or else your color card is red!"

Evaluation of a Discipline Plan

Determining the effectiveness of a discipline plan is not simple. Counting the number of referrals or the frequency of misbehavior can be helpful, but such procedures often give a one-dimensional snapshot of a three-dimensional problem. A discipline plan that reduces incidents of misbehavior can be a disaster if it also reduces student motivation and learning. When evaluating the effectiveness of any discipline plan, teachers and administrators must include the following questions with any numerical data relating to incidents of misbehavior:

Figure 2.3
Responsibility Model of Discipline

Main goal: To teach students to make responsible choices.

Principle: To learn from the outcomes of decisions.

Consequences:

Internal locus

Done *by* the student

Logical or natural

Examples

   • Developing a plan describing how you will behave without breaking the rule when you are in a similar situation

   • Practicing appropriate behavior in a private meeting with the teacher

Student learns . . .

   • I cause my own outcomes.

   • I have more than one alternative behavior in any situation.

   • I have the power to choose the best alternative.

---

1. What happens to the student 10 minutes after an intervention? Is she angry? Is she back to the lesson? Do you see signs of passive-aggressive behavior? Is she fully participating?

2. What happens to the student the next day?

3. What happens to the student a week later?

4. What happens to student motivation? Does energy for learning increase or decrease? (Good discipline plans enhance student motivation; they do not erode it.)

5. What happens to the student's dignity? Is it attacked? Is it maintained? Is it enhanced?

6. How is the student's locus of control affected? An internal orientation, when appropriate, leads to responsibility (e.g., "What I did wasn't right, and I feel bad about it"). An external

orientation leads to blame and helplessness (e.g., "It wasn't me. Everyone does it, but you always pick on me. She did it first").

7. What happens to the teacher-student relationship? Is communication improved? Is it weakened? Did the teacher win the battle (get the student to do what the teacher wanted) but lose the war (destroy their delicate relationship)?

8. Does the student learn about his behavior in a way that provides increased choices, or does the student learn that he has no choice at all? Choices lead to responsibility.

In Conclusion

Effective discipline does not come from the quick mastery of techniques or the implementation of a packaged method. Effective discipline comes from the heart and soul of the teacher. It comes from the belief that teaching students to take responsibility for their behavior is as much the "job" of the teacher as teaching history or math and more important than simply enforcing rules. It comes from the belief that most students do the best they can, many in what they feel is an adverse environment. It comes from the belief that all students need hope. It comes from the positive energy of the teacher. Only within the framework of the teacher's internal strength and the development of a hopeful and caring classroom environment can a discipline plan be effective. Good discipline requires proper attitudes that guide effective strategies.

3

The Three Key Dimensions

❧ WHAT WE HAVE LEARNED ❧

This chapter provides the basic framework for the Discipline with Dignity approach to classroom management. In it, we identify and explain the three dimensions of discipline: prevention, action, and resolution. A major aspect of the Discipline with Dignity approach is the belief that discipline problems are most often the result of one or more unfulfilled basic needs that lead students to act in unacceptable ways. Preventing problems from occurring or recurring is best done through classroom strategies and practices designed to address these basic needs. In the first edition, we implied the importance of having a student-centered approach that addressed basic needs, but we did not articulate what these needs were. Since then, we have spoken and written extensively about these basic needs (Mendler, 2005; Mendler & Curwin, 1999).

School policy and classroom rules need to recognize the internal forces that motivate students to act inappropriately. In formulating school policy or classroom strategy, we may find it helpful to think of three Cs:

- Connection
- Competence
- Control

Does the strategy provide students with a greater sense of connection, competence, or control? We have found that disruptive students invariably have problems because one or more of these needs are unfulfilled. They feel *unconnected* to the mainstream of what school has to offer, *unable* to success-fully achieve, or *incapable* of feeling that anybody much cares about their opinion or perspective. By contrast, well-functioning students generally feel connected to the main goal of school: academic success. They feel confident enough to believe that with adequate effort, they will be sufficiently successful. Furthermore, most believe they "matter" to peers and adults. Effective disci-pline is about addressing these needs so that all students believe they can be successful and feel they matter to important others.

A student with the unfulfilled need for *connection* is most likely to seek attention from others. If she cannot get this through appropriate actions, she is likely to say or do things that will get her noticed. Students most often make this need known by saying silly things, making noises, and bothering others.

When students have issues with *competence*, they tend to give up easily or act out when presented with material they find too challenging. The refrains most prominent in the vocabulary of these students are "This is stupid" and "I don't care." What they are really saying is "I feel stupid (so why bother trying)," and "I am afraid to care (because if I did I probably wouldn't do very well anyway, and then I would really feel stupid)." To complicate matters, it is not uncommon for them to reject work designed to promote success as "too easy." Other students are afraid of success. They believe that success will place an undo burden on them for further success. Many of these students prefer to fail, which keeps expectations low.

When problems occur from students with *control* issues, these usually take the form of power struggles. They feel a strong need to argue and take charge. Such students often act bossy and disrespectful. Deep down, they worry that they do not really matter, so they are constantly doing things in an effort to influence others.

Missing in the discipline plans of most schools and classrooms is attention to prevention. At least as important as rules and consequences is a specific plan that articulates what the teacher will do on a daily basis with the whole class, with selected groups of troubled students, and with individuals to help them feel more connected, competent, and in control. This plan works best when it is integrated into a teacher's plan for discipline that includes values, rules, and consequences. Figure 3.1 provides an example.

Figure 3.1
Weekly Class Plan for Discipline Prevention

Connection

 Every day I will be at the door to greet each student.

 I will ask an opinion of at least two students who rarely contribute.

 I will invite two tough students to have lunch with me at least once.

Competence

 At least twice this week, I will help Carlos, Joanne, and Mary (three of my lowest-functioning students) to earn A's by comparing their current work to their past work if they make an academic improvement.

 I will give the class at least two open book quizzes at the beginning of class so that all students on time and with their books can earn A's.

 I will give each student at least one opportunity to redo, revise, or retake an assignment or test to improve a grade.

Control

 I will give meaningful choices within each assignment to all students.

 If a difficult student breaks a rule, before I decide on a consequence, I will first ask the student what would help the student not break the rule again. I will do this at least one time.

 I will invite a difficult student to help me solve either a class or school problem involving challenging behavior.

 Effective discipline is about constructing a school or classroom that encourages curriculum, activities, and interactions to address the basic needs of connection, competence, and control. Consider the following examples:

• George Nelson continually yells during the day. Kicking children out and sending students to in-school suspension does not work, yet he finds himself resorting to escalating threats to try to get the class to follow his rules.

• Sally Aldredge states very clear rules and tells her students what will happen when rules are violated. But Sally carries out her consequences only when she is in a bad mood and usually only with the students she dislikes. When her favorite students break the rules, she reminds them with a slightly hidden smile that if they "do that again, they will have to . . . ."

• Joan Stevenson took a course in behavior modification and learned how to set up a contingency program in her class. Her principal supported the concept and even brought in a consultant who worked with five teachers to set up model programs. Unfortunately, Joan's plan failed. No one bothered to tell her that because her value system was opposed to the philosophy of behavior modification, the plan would not work for her. Joan felt like a failure when the consultant told her that behavior modification was a "proven method" that worked if correctly applied. She hadn't learned that one must believe in what one does in order for any approach or technique to "work."

• Tom Wilson has few problems with most of his students, but he has two students who continually drive him crazy. He has noticed an increase in the number and intensity of headaches he has when he goes home and has taken to carrying his bottle of ibuprofen throughout the day. None of the traditional approaches has worked with these two students, and because the school will not suspend them, Tom must face them almost daily. Unfortunately for Tom, these students are rarely absent.

These teachers and thousands like them all suffer from one basic problem. They do not have an established plan or system for implementing a discipline policy that is consistent with their needs and with the needs of their students. The result is a sinking feeling of helplessness and despair, blaming students, administrators, and professors of education.

Discipline with Dignity focuses on three key dimensions of classroom management that integrate many theoretical approaches developed by educators and psychologists who value maintaining student dignity and teaching responsible behavior.

• **Prevention:** what the teacher can do to actively prevent discipline problems and to deal with the stress associated with classroom disruptions.

• **Action:** what actions the teacher can take when, in spite of all the steps taken to prevent discipline problems, they still occur. The focus is on stopping misbehavior quickly in a dignified way while keeping the misbehaving student in class so that the teacher can get back to teaching. The goal is to keep minor problems from escalating into major ones. By stopping a problem in a dignified way, the teacher is also helping ensure that it is less likely to recur.

• **Resolution:** what the teacher can do to resolve issues with the chronic rule breaker and the more extreme, "out-of-control" student or at least to diminish the intense negative impact such students have on the teaching-learning process.

The Prevention Dimension

The first goal of the three-dimensional approach (Figure 3.2) is to set up an environment in which discipline problems are prevented. Teachers have two different mind-sets when it comes to discipline: intervention and prevention. Intervention, the most common, assumes students are going to misbehave and thinks about what to do after it happens. Here is an example of an intervention mind-set: A teacher writes a number on the board that indicates the amount of play minutes the students get at the end of the day. Every time a student does something disruptive or inappropriate, a minute is removed. This mind-set basically says, "I'm just waiting for you to screw up. And when you do, I will be ready to catch you." This type of teacher creates fear inside the classroom. Students become afraid to make mistakes and walk around on pins and needles all day. Other students satiate on minutes taken away and tell you they don't care. Some students even bet on who can lose the most minutes.

Figure 3.2
The Three Dimensions of Discipline Overview

Prevention Dimension

What Can Be Done to Prevent Discipline Problems:

1. Know and express yourself clearly.

2. Know your students.

3. Make your classroom a motivating place.

4. Teach responsibility and caring.

5. Establish effective rules and consequences.

6. Keep yourself current.

7. Deal with stressful conflict.

Action Dimension

What to Do When Discipline Problems Occur:

1. Stop the misbehavior quickly.

2. Get back to teaching.

3. Keep students in class.

4. Implement consequence.

5. Collect data.

Resolution Dimension

1. Find what is needed to prevent another problem.

2. Develop mutually agreeable plan.

3. Implement plan.

4. Monitor plan/revise if necessary.

5. Use creative/unconventional approaches when necessary.

The prevention mind-set is very different. It assumes students are going to behave appropriately and looks for ways to generate success. This mind-set gets students looking for positive things to do. Prevention starts with defining the difference between fair and equal. For example, tell your class:

> I just want to let you all know right now that you will not all be getting the same assignment or even the same test because my job is to help each of you get better today than you were yesterday in this subject. Some of us are better at math right now than others, but all of us can get better than we were yesterday. So if you get a different test or assignment than someone else, that's why. Some of you may not yet have learned proper manners and might even say rude, nasty or inappropriate things to each other. If it happens, sometimes I will give a consequence to one person that is different from one I give to another if I think different people will learn better behavior from a different consequence. [See Chapter 5 for more on this topic.]
>
> I also want to tell you right now that I will only talk to you about you this year. So if you have a complaint, let me know what you think will work better for you. I will not discuss anyone else's grades, assignments, consequences, or anything else. I'm sure you would not want me to talk about you behind your back, which is why I will not be talking to you about anyone else behind theirs. However, I will always talk to you about you. So if you are thinking about complaining about someone else, remember: I'm not discussing anyone else with you.

Prevention is so important when working with tough students. Begin to take that mind-set and start thinking ahead. Teaching becomes much easier.

We think of the prevention dimension as similar to a subject curriculum. The best curricula are goal directed but flexible enough to allow day-to-day changes as new needs arise. They incorporate evaluations of how well the plan is working. The prevention dimension provides structure and direction but is sufficiently flexible to accommodate both day-to-day and long-term changes as you and your students develop new needs and new awareness.

The prevention dimension has seven stages. Let's take a closer look at each one.

Stage 1: Know and Express Yourself Clearly

The first stage of the prevention dimension is to know yourself so that you can communicate your thoughts, feelings, routines, and procedures clearly. Some classroom discipline problems occur because of double messages that the teacher gives the students. For example, Mrs. Jones, a 4th grade teacher, wants to be liked by her students. She has trouble understanding why her children are so rowdy and rarely listen to her. Unfortunately, she is unaware of her soft tone of voice and nonassertive body posture when she tells them to line up or open their books. She is afraid they will think she is mean if she raises her voice. Mrs. Jones, without being aware, is constantly sending double messages. Her verbal message states anger, while her nonverbal message expresses her wish for the students to like her. Mixed signals often lead to agitation and anxiety in students, culminating in conflict, confusion, and classroom management problems.

A reality rarely faced directly by educators is that there are some students we just do not like. In life, it is OK to have preferences for some people over others. It is good to acknowledge at least to yourself and perhaps to a trusted colleague who these children are. Yet on "company time," we must get past the feelings of frustration and dread that often accompany working with difficult students. Try seeing a student who seems not to try despite your best efforts as a child who is overwhelmed by the fear of failure.

Things can change dramatically when an "oppositional defiant student" is seen as a "tenacious leader." It enables us to respond in a much more encouraging way. For example, "Joey, I know I cannot *force* you to do your work because you have a strong mind of your own, but I can *ask* you to do a few problems because if you do not, I won't know if I am being a good teacher. So consider yourself asked. Thanks for doing either the first three or the last three." We are much more likely to influence change in difficult students when we invite rather than force them to let go of the familiar.

Sharing your feelings with a trusted colleague can provide some cathartic relief that can be healthy in itself. We are reminded of Jack Washington, a senior high teacher who always appeared uptight. When asked to imagine his most troublesome class in front of him and to express his feelings, he laughed, saying, "That 'shrink' stuff won't work with me." After some moderate encouragement, including telling him that this type of strategy was sometimes used to help major league ballplayers improve their performance, Jack tried the technique. Soon he was crying, sharing a long-standing feeling of inadequacy. After three sessions like this, Jack learned some alternative methods of expressing his feelings. Eventually he was better able to deal with his feelings of helplessness that were in direct conflict with his macho self-image. A month later he reported enjoying teaching more than at any other time in his life.

To help you see the connection between expressing feelings and successful classroom teaching, try keeping a simple journal for one week. The following sample questions and answers can serve as a model for this experiment. Take two or three minutes each morning before your first class, just before lunch, and immediately after your last class to answer the questions.

Monday

Morning: Right now I feel (fill in any four words)

1. _____ 2. _____ 3. _____ 4. _____

Circle the strongest feeling.

Write one sentence about the strongest feeling.

Noon: (Repeat format.)

End of day: (Repeat format.)

Once you have completed your format for one week, answer the following questions:

1. How many words would you classify as positive? How many as negative?

2. How many of your circled words would you classify as positive? How many as negative?

3. Were your feelings more positive in the morning, afternoon, or at the end of the day?

4. Do you see any patterns in your feelings?

5. What methods do you use to express, acknowledge, or deal with your positive feelings about your teaching? Be specific.

6. What methods do you use to express, acknowledge, or deal with your negative feelings about your teaching? Be specific.

7. Think of a student who is difficult for you to handle. What words characterize this student? Are these words mostly positive or negative? If they are primarily negative, can you think of positive word substitutes? Next time you have a demand of this student, imagine approaching him or her as if this student displays these more positive characteristics. What would you say and how would you say it?

The process of knowing and expressing yourself clearly need not be exhausting or particularly time-consuming. We invite you to reflect on the suggestions in Figure 3.3 to see what you think you might change that could lead to more effective behavior management.

Stage 2: Know Your Students

The second stage of the prevention dimension is knowing what makes your students tick. The needs and desires of your students play a major role in developing a preventive environment.

We recently saw a teacher disciplining a student in a 5th grade class. When the teacher asked the student if he understood her, he did a very quick upward movement with his head. In this instance that small movement meant yes. The teacher,

---

Figure 3.3
About My Practices Survey

Read the following statements and decide which you think you do the right amount of and which you think it might be good to do more of to prevent discipline problems.

I usually correct behavior in a dignified way.

I encourage students to work independently in self-directed activities.

I find ways to like my students who try to make themselves unlikable.

I allow my students to make some decisions about classroom management.

I allow my students to openly disagree with me.

I greet students regularly.

I laugh a lot in class.

I regularly connect with my difficult students around something that interests them.

I allow students to redo, retake, and revise their work to improve their grades.

When I have a problem with a student, I take some responsibility for contributing to it.

I call parents at least twice to share something positive before I seek help with a problem.

I have a suggestion box in my class and ask students to contribute ideas that they think will make the class an even better place.

I take time to tell my students what they do that I like, and to ask them to tell me what they like about others and myself.

I give my students some say in curriculum content.

My students are involved in developing rules and consequences.

Now take one statement you want to do more of and list three specific steps you can take to do more of it.

---

not feeling satisfied with the response, asked him again, this time in a firmer tone. The student, now visibly upset, said, "I already said yes, bitch." A power struggle ensued, and the student was removed from class. Recognizing the nonverbal message might have prevented this incident from escalating.

Here are some other common nonverbal student behaviors:

• **Shoulder shrug.** Shrugging quickly upward means the student is not sure. In this instance, give her a chance to think about her answer. Or simply move on to another student.

• **A student milling around your room.** This activity usually means the student needs to talk to you but is not sure how to begin the conversation. A simple "How's it going" or "So what's on your mind?" is a good ice breaker.

• **Eye contact.** We often hear teachers say, "You look at me when I'm talking to you." However, in life when we are uncomfortable in a situation, our natural instinct is to look away. It is not realistic to expect eye contact until after you've established a relationship with a student. In some cultures, strong eye contact is a sign of disrespect. Some students will make quick eye contact and then look away. This also usually means yes.

The more aware you are of your students, their surroundings, their culture, and their home life, the more *connected* they will feel.

When we welcome and greet students regularly or spend an extra few seconds to ask or address something pertinent about their day, they begin to believe the classroom is a good place to be. When we take time to teach impulsive students how to quiet themselves or struggling students methods to solve an equation, their *competence* is enhanced. Figure 3.3 can help you assess the degree to which you do the kinds of things you value that could enhance your classroom management skills.

There are many activities you can use to become more aware of your students that take little time and promote a positive classroom climate. Mendler (2001) offers strategies that teachers can use daily to connect with their students. We advise you to familiarize yourself with all of your students through a cursory glance at their school records. When you discover students who have had an unhappy or unsuccessful prior school experience, it is wise to find out more about those students' interests or hobbies so that you become able to connect with them in a way that promotes positive feelings. If, for example, you know that Howie has been unsuccessful and disruptive in the last several math classes and you teach math, and if you discover that he enjoys baseball, you might greet him with a discussion of yesterday's baseball scores. Nowadays, it is wise to know at least a little bit about sports, music, and video games. Many of our students spend lots of time listening to their iPods and playing video games, so keeping ourselves informed by dipping our toes in their interests makes us relevant to them. The following questions can help us focus on things to do that may prevent problems from occurring or continuing:

1. Think of a student who seems to disrupt class to gain the attention of others or who always seems to be doing something to draw attention. What kinds of things can you see yourself doing in the classroom that might help this student get noticed by others before he acts out?

2. Think of a student who seems to misbehave more when you put her in an academically demanding situation. Can you think of some ways you might present the material to encourage success? What might happen if you had her do fewer problems? Are there things you might regularly say to encourage success? Can you think of some situations where she might actually be able to tutor a younger or disabled student? Might it be possible for you to tell the student in advance which question you will be calling on her to answer, and then give her the answer so she is sure to get it right?

3. Do you have students in your class who always feel the need to be in charge? It may seem as if they are constantly trying to usurp your authority. What things might you do to make them see themselves as leaders or decision makers in your class? Something as simple as regularly asking for their opinion can help. We met one teacher who put her most talkative and disruptive 4th grader on "noise patrol." His job every day was getting the class to be quiet after lunch.

Figure 3.4 is designed to illustrate the importance of knowing who your students are and gaining valuable information from them.

Stage 3: Make Your Classroom a Motivating Place

It is impossible to force students to learn. We can quiet them down or stop them from disrupting others, but discipline will never replace motivating activities or effective teaching methods. By connecting to the natural motivation of students, teachers can prevent many discipline problems. Although there are many ways to motivate, inspiration, enthusiasm, and challenge are the keys.

Get your students to believe in their endless possibilities. A wonderful story in *USA Today* (Fisher, 2007) profiled Jeff Lewis, a high school math teacher in Mesa, Arizona, where he has taught for 29 years. Due to a rare blood infection, Jeff became a quadruple amputee a few years ago and now has prosthetic arms and legs. The story noted that he had recently completed a 4.2-mile race, frequently goes bowling, and occasionally wears shorts to school to show what prostheses look like. The article quoted his students as saying things like, "He is a funny, funny man. . . . Some teachers can be sourpusses but not Mr. Lewis. He out of all people should be, but he doesn't let his difficulties get to him. . . . Mr. Lewis always makes geometry fun. You can never guess what will happen because he is so unpredictable." Lewis offers his students and others this advice: "Do not be a spectator. Life is 10% what happens to you and 90% how you respond to it."

Mendler (2001), Curwin (2006), Ciaccio (2004), and Rogers (1999) offer very practical guides with many tips that can get and keep students motivated. Chapter 9 provides important keys to motivating students along with several strategies.

Figure 3.4
Student Knowledge Inventory

Write the name of one of your favorite students on the top of Column 1 and the name of one of your least favorite students on the top of Column 2. Answer the related questions about each student as best you can.

Most Favorite Student	**Least Favorite Student**
Favorite in-school activity:	
Favorite hobby:	
Favorite television show:	
Favorite music group or video game:	
Best friend (name):	
One thing this student likes about your class:	
One thing this student dislikes about your class:	
One short-range goal:	
One long-range goal:	
One skill he or she is most proud of:	

Figure 3.4—(*continued*)
Student Knowledge Inventory

Questions

1. Which student do I know more about?

2. Which student do I spend more positive time with?

3. What specific steps might I take to interact more positively with my difficult students?

    a. I will _____

    b. I will _____

    c. I will _____

4. What might I do less of with difficult students to get to better know their strengths?

    a. I will _____

    b. I will _____

    c. I will _____

For one week, keep a record of how often you do your six "I wills". See if anything changes.

Change You Expected:

Positive: _____

_____

Negative: _____

_____

Change That Was Unexpected:

Positive: _____

_____

Negative: _____

_____

Stage 4: Teach Responsibility and Caring

The best ongoing way to promote responsibility is to have students involved in as many decisions as possible. Giving them manageable choices within homework, test questions, and even topics of study helps enhance decision-making skills. Getting them involved in deciding on a proper consequence for an infraction teaches responsibility. For example, "Hidalgo, talking out of turn makes it hard for me to give everyone a chance. We've talked before about this, and it is still a problem. What do you plan to do to solve this problem, because I would prefer that you handle it rather than me? What consequence do you think would be fair in case you forget to follow your plan?"

Asking their opinion about curricula or cosmetic matters and getting them to do for others are additional ways of teaching responsibility. Responsibility can also be enhanced in behavior modification programs by involving students in monitoring and reinforcing their own behaviors.

Stage 5: Establish Effective Rules and Consequences (Social Contracts)

The fifth aspect of prevention involves establishing social contracts with your class. A *social contract* is a list of values, rules, and consequences that define proper behavior deemed necessary for good learning and teaching to occur (see Chapter 4). A value (e.g., "We solve our problems peacefully") is necessarily broader than a rule because its purpose is to provide the reason for why we need to have rules. Obviously, *peaceful problem solving* is a value because learning and teaching will not occur if students and teaches feel unsafe. It generally works best when teachers identify the school and/or classroom values and then involve students in defining the rules. In most school districts, key values are often defined at the level of the school board and are contained along with rules in a policy manual.

We encourage schools and teachers to use these points as a good start toward developing classroom rules and expectations. For example, the classroom/school values might be as follows:

Take care of yourself.
Take care of each other.
Take care of this place.

The teacher may then offer specific examples of rules that are guided by each of these values (e.g., "Pick up litter even if you didn't leave it"). Students are strongly encouraged to propose specific rules as well. Encourage discussion seeking consensus. Variations of social contracts include having students propose rules for the teacher as well as for each other. The teacher might say, "I'd like to know what you think I could or should do that will best help you learn. Come up with a rule or two that you would like to see me follow." This process is explained more fully in Chapter 4.

Whether or not students are directly involved in developing rules, specific procedures associated with success need to be identified in order for the classroom to be a predictable place (see Figure 3.5).

Stage 6: Keep Yourself Current

The sixth component of prevention is learning about child behavior, theories of discipline, and some of the research into psychology and education as it applies to discipline. For example, Charles (2008) offers an overview of various theories and strategies related to discipline and classroom management. Knowledge alone will not make you a better classroom manager, but knowledge can generate alternatives. For example, a relatively new frontier in working with ADHD students is the use of exercise to manage behavior. For reasons only beginning to be understood, movement can be used to get students more focused. One of the authors has had considerable success in getting ADHD students better focused on activities requiring sitting, looking, and listening by giving each a pedometer and having them track the number of steps they take during prescribed periods of movement. The goal is for each student to progressively move faster during these short intervals of only a few minutes. Similar activities have included brisk walks through the building and the use of music stands that allow students to stand while working. The value of keeping current is particularly useful when working with especially difficult students who often do not respond to conventional approaches. Much more on unconventional teaching methods is shared in Chapter 8.

Figure 3.5
Procedures Checklist

Before teaching a lesson, it is important to consider what procedures students will need to know. Proper behavior usually requires that you teach and regularly review details regarding each of the following. Make this a checklist of reminders for yourself:

1. How to enter the class appropriately

2. Where to put completed assignments

3. What to do when they enter the classroom

4. Where to find the daily assignment

5. How to get permission to leave the room

6. How to quickly join their work group

7. How to get your attention when they need it and you are working with somebody else

8. What to do when someone says or does something mean to them

9. How to express themselves when they disagree with you

10. How to acceptably leave at the end of class

11. What to do when they are stuck and need help

12. What to do after they have completed a class assignment but before others have finished

What other procedures or expectations of small details do your students need to know that are important to the success of your lesson(s)?

Stage 7: Deal with Stressful Conflict

The final stage of prevention is stress management. It is about teaching our students and ourselves how to remain calm when people push our buttons. Many discipline problems occur because stressed-out teachers are trying to get stressed-out kids to do what they want. Some occur because students or teachers bring their life stress into the classroom, and it impacts what is said and done. Chapter 7 offers several stress management methods that help diffuse tension so that discipline problems are less likely to occur.

The Action Dimension

Despite all your efforts at prevention, conflicts inevitably occur in any setting where several people are together over an extended period of time. The purpose of the action dimension is to stop misbehavior quickly so that teaching can resume with a minimal loss of instruction. In short, we want to quickly get back to teaching without requiring the student to leave unless his presence continues to interrupt the learning process. Finally, the action needs to preserve both the teacher's and student's dignity, and it must be something that does not diminish the teacher's classroom authority.

In addition to stopping the misbehavior, implementation of a consequence is often required and is therefore part of the action dimension. Most often, a simple reminder is all that is needed. For example, "Nancy, thanks for discarding the gum right now and remembering to follow this rule in the future." There are four types of consequences (see Chapter 5 for a detailed discussion of each):

- Natural and logical: those that are directly related to the behavior (e.g., you make a mess, you clean it up)
- Conventional: improving those that already exist (e.g., making detention more meaningful)

- Generic: those that apply to every rule
- Educational: those that teach new behaviors

The method of implementation is at least as important as the consequence itself. Tone of voice, degree of physical distance from the student, body posture, eye contact, and other nonverbal gestures determine the effectiveness of a consequence as much or more than the actual content of the consequence itself. Sensitivity to personal, cultural, and emotional issues is necessary when successfully stopping misbehavior. Merely implementing a consequence in a rote, unfeeling way can become mechanical and dehumanize the whole Discipline with Dignity approach. Similarly, too much emotion or lecturing can undermine the effectiveness of a consequence. Stay away from a scolding expository such as "Nancy, there is no gum chewing in this class. You know the rules. The first violation is a reminder. This is your reminder, young lady!"

The prevention and action dimensions take care of most classroom discipline problems. Only the more troublesome and chronic problems will persist once the first two dimensions are implemented.

The Resolution Dimension

The resolution dimension is comprised of activities designed to reach the most difficult and challenging students. Most of these students have already lost hope and have been overexposed and desensitized to many school and classroom discipline interventions. If you threaten them with detention, many will say, "So what? I already have a ton of detentions to serve. All my friends will be there." If you warn them that they will fail the test if they do not study, many shrug, having failed most of the tests they have ever taken. They expect to routinely get kicked out of class, sent to the principal's office, or suspended. Calling home is rarely effective because many either are raising their parents or have convinced parents that school people are jerks.

Reaching these students requires a great deal of effort with little assurance that there will ever be a payoff. Some teachers wonder if it is even worth the effort to try, given the disproportionate time that they consume. Obviously, every educator must decide how much energy to invest in chronically disruptive students. We know that those we do not reach are at a much higher risk of committing crimes or otherwise being drains on society. So although they take more time and creativity, reaching and influencing them is immensely important.

We offer many alternatives that have the potential for reaching chronically challenging students in Chapters 8 and 10. Most of these strategies are considered "unconventional" because they are not normally included in school policies or recommended practices.

One payoff for the teacher who is willing to try creative approaches is the opportunity to experiment with techniques that are generally considered too radical for the mainstream. Eventually, many of these techniques expand the teacher's awareness of possibilities to teach all children and generate new energy because of the challenge of experimenting with the unexpected. Those who have developed their ability to reach particularly difficult students often become master teachers.

For the Administrator

The Discipline with Dignity approach is a broad-based program flexible enough to fit all schools and most teachers. As the administrator in your building, it is important for you to accept that your faculty is diverse, has a variety of values, and uses a multitude of strategies when managing student behavior. In the same way you might suggest that a teacher begins by working with student strengths, you can begin helping your teachers by identifying their own unique strengths in relation to discipline. Talk to them individually about what you think they are good at. Some teachers are outstanding lecturers. Others are good at

facilitating group work. Encourage them to focus on these qualities while improving other areas that might make them better
teachers. Improvement in classroom management can be built
upon these strengths.

The School Discipline Survey (see Appendix B) can be a
useful tool when working with faculty and staff to discover how
much agreement and disagreement exists on issues related to
discipline. Areas with large discrepancies can cause morale
problems and confuse students. Areas with great agreement are
sources of strength on which to build. You can use the survey
at the beginning of the school year or at the end of the previous
year to analyze how to improve school discipline.

To ensure that your teachers receive the support they want
and perhaps expect from you, ask each teacher to discuss his
or her plans with you for preventing discipline problems from
occurring. Suggest that, at the least, teachers provide you with
details of their values, rules, and consequences early in the
school year so that both you and they are clear about what is
expected. Be sure that the rules and consequences are compatible with the school's mission and values. Let teachers know
generally what you consider to be valid and less valid reasons to
involve you in classroom discipline issues.

To facilitate the process of teachers seeing the benefits of
broader knowledge of themselves and their students, you can
present the About My Practices Survey (Figure 3.3) and the
Student Knowledge Inventory (Figure 3.4) at one of your faculty
meetings. Feel free to adapt these tools to include questions or
themes that might be more relevant to your school's circumstances. We suggest inviting your teachers to develop methods
according to four criteria:

- Does it work?
- Does it preserve a person's dignity, or does it humiliate?
- Does it teach responsibility, or does it rely exclusively on
obedience?
- How does it affect motivation to learn?

Emphasize the importance of relationship building. Disruptive, difficult, and unmotivated students are often looking for someone to follow. Give your teachers ideas for how to build these relationships as well as the time to do so. Have open discussions about cultural differences and how they relate to nonverbal communication. Many administrators are afraid to broach this subject.

In many of the schools where we do training and staff development, neighborhoods are changing, in some cases dramatically. Often test scores are lower than before. These changes are occasionally creating fear, misunderstanding, blame, and confusion among school personnel. Administrators can offer comfort, training, emotional security, tolerance, and strong leadership to help their staff recognize and adjust to these changes.

Much of this book is about sharing methods that work, preserve dignity, emphasize responsibility, and do not adversely affect motivation to learn. We have found that schools with the most effective discipline and strongest faculty support are those with an active principal who respects staff and student diversity. The principal is a leader who sets the tone by having clear, consistent rules and is unafraid of holding staff accountable. The active principal is visible in the halls, in the cafeteria, and at the bus stop and greets the staff and knows students' names. Such a principal wants to go into the classroom to spell a teacher because that principal wants direct, positive, instructional contact with staff and students. A "we," not "me," feeling is encouraged through listening and reacting to the individual and collective thoughts of the school community.

4

The Social Contract

Social contract is the term we use to define the process of teachers and students developing values, rules, and consequences. Over the years many teachers have told us that the social contract has helped save their careers. When we first introduced these concepts, they were considered revolutionary. Now they are recommended by most other programs dealing with student behavior. In *The Discipline Book* (Curwin & Mendler, 1980), we first proposed the importance of involving students in the process of making and enforcing rules and consequences to give them a sense of ownership. Later we understood the need to base all rules and consequences on values.

We remain firm advocates for involving students as decision makers. The beauty of doing so is that it shows that everyone's voice is valued and worthy of being heard. This is therefore an excellent way to positively address a student's need for control. Sadly, in too many places, children feel that nobody really cares about what they think. The social contract is one important way to convey to students that we respect their ideas and opinions. In fact, we believe that most schools place far too much emphasis on rules and consequences as the solution to discipline problems. Invariably, a school committee meets to address behavioral concerns and often gets bogged down trying to figure out how to get all staff on the same page. New rules and so-called consequences (which usually are really punishments and, in some cases, rewards) are developed, shared, and written into the school handbook with the expectation that everybody will now do things the same way. Members of the committee feel a sense of accomplishment and hope that their work will have a favorable impact on student behavior.

Unfortunately, in most cases, this process fails to really improve discipline at school for two reasons. The first reason is that is there are differences among staff in how much they value the rules and consequences, and therefore not everybody enforces them. The second reason is that too much emphasis has been placed on rules and consequences to fix problems, with an insufficient emphasis on such powerful factors that can influence change as the teacher-student relationship, relevance of the curriculum, and ways for students to believe in their capacity for success.

Most important, good discipline is viewing students as individuals with ideas, opinions, and feelings. We must trust them as capable associates when invited to share ideas and solve problems. It is important then to run the classroom in a manner compatible with this view. We offer the process of developing a social contract as one important means to this end.

Not all of the specific steps we present in this chapter are necessary for all teachers to follow. For example, in the original publication, we emphasized the importance of giving a test for comprehension of the rules and consequences and then tying the earning of all classroom privileges to passing the test with a 100 percent score. Although this approach remains recommended as a way to eliminate the "I didn't know" excuse some students use when they get caught, many teachers have used the essence of the social contract as a way of importantly sharing decision-making ownership with their students without giving a test for comprehension.

One key aspect of discipline we failed to address in the first edition was the importance of having clear procedures about basic daily tasks such as how to enter and leave a classroom, where to find missed assignments when absent, and how to go about turning in papers without disruption. Since then, Wong and Wong (2004) and Smith (2004), among others, have addressed this shortcoming and offer many useful suggestions for educators. Student involvement in the process of developing and enforcing values, rules, and consequences can be a valuable component of effective discipline, particularly when implemented by knowledgeable, stimulating teachers who come across as caring and in charge.

The *social contract* is an agreement between teacher and students about the values, rules, and consequences for classroom behavior. The basic design of the social contract is establishing rules and consequences based on guiding principles or values. The keys to developing an effective social contract are as follows:

- Connect rules to values/principles.
- Identify rules needed to run an effective classroom.
- Involve students in developing rules for what they believe they need from you and each other to be successful.
- Ensure that rules are clear and specific.
- Make consequences relate as directly to the rule as possible (more on this in Chapter 5).
- In developing a consequence, be guided primarily by what is likely to be learned by the student to improve behavior, not by delivering misery.
- Develop a predictable range of consequences for rule violations that allow teachers to match one of many alternative consequences to a particular circumstance.
- If a student or parent thinks a different consequence will be more effective to change behavior, consider going along with the change and holding the student or parent accountable.
- In developing rules and consequences, err on the side of what is educationally sound rather than what is politically correct.
- Update the contract regularly to ensure effectiveness.

The social contract is patterned after our democratic decision-making system of government, which has been shown to be an effective model in schools, although it is within the context of the teacher being in charge. White and Lippitt's (1960) classic studies of 10- and 11-year-old children showed that an authoritarian teacher approach led to high work output by children but was accompanied by aggression directed at the teacher. Children in democratic groups that were guided by the teachers but also clearly involved the students in decision making had nearly as high a work output, got along "best" with the teacher, and worked slightly better than the authoritarian group when the teacher was out of the room. Children with laissez-faire teachers did worst on all criteria. More recently, several researchers (e.g., Beane, 2005; Hursh & Ross, 2000) have noted the social and academic benefits of growing democracy in classrooms by meaningfully involving students.

Be Aware of the System Effect

The social contract is a system of values, rules, and consequences. Although systems are necessary to provide structure and guidelines, we must never feel enslaved by them. The system should exist to serve the person rather than the person always being required to fit into the system. Two attitudes make sure the social contract system serves students most effectively:

• Instead of saying, "If I do it for you, I'll have to do it for everyone," try "Let me see if I can make this work for you without making everyone else unhappy."

• Instead of saying, "This is the system we use, and there is nothing I can do about it," try "This is our system. Let's see how we can make it work to help you."

Students from all social and ability groups can become cynical, unmotivated, alienated, or hostile when they perceive the system doesn't care about them. They will often take out their frustrations, either actively or passive-aggressively, by striking back at every opportunity. Students like this feel gratified by beating the system, or even by attempting to do so, and all the reasons and rationality for maintaining order become meaningless. The more they are told by those who represent the system that they are violating policy, the more they have bolstered their dignity.

Systems are not malicious. The way people use them determines whether they are helpful or a roadblock to human interaction. For example, let's examine the large supermarket and the small neighborhood grocer. The large supermarket offers lower prices and more choices. It has a larger staff and access to computer technology. It makes deals with large food companies that the corner store cannot. Yet, when a store loses its humanity and its ability to make customers feel that their special needs will be met, patrons are resentful. The corner store has higher prices and less selection, but the owner knows most patrons by name and takes time out of his day to ask about the family. He personally shows the customer daily specials and even offers a sample of something new. When his customer finishes shopping, the corner grocer says, "Come back soon"—and means it. Both the large supermarket and the neighborhood store have a system.

When students see the classroom as the large supermarket that values efficiency over humanity, many will fight back. When they perceive the classroom as the corner store, they feel welcome and valued. Nearly every school has at least one or two teachers who have earned the respect of the toughest students. When asked why they like these teachers, the students say things like "He treats me as a human"; "She treats me with respect"; "He cares about me as a person, not just as a student"; "She listens"; "He doesn't tell me what to do all the time"; "She gives me the chance to make my own decisions"; and "He believes in me—he believes that I can succeed." These teachers have systems that guide what they and their students do rather than try to control what they do.

The social contract is a system designed to enhance human interaction in the classroom. The social contract process includes shared decision making, the opportunity for change, and the chance to see situations in their natural complexity rather than to simplify them down to "easily manageable levels."

This approach also builds in the potential for inefficiency and human mistakes, but in the long run, the classroom environment is enhanced by working through problem situations rather than letting a system make the decision.

Suggested Procedure for Developing a Social Contract

There is no one correct way to create a social contract. Teachers are encouraged to make the social contract fit their own styles and situations. The following features are most often represented:

- Classroom values or principles
- Specific rules that are based on the values/principles
- A range of consequences for each rule
- Student input developing rules and consequences
- A test for student comprehension
- A time investment
- Communication with parents
- Use of administrators

Sound Principles and Values

As previously mentioned, values or principles (the terms are used interchangeably here) place rules in a larger context that helps students understand why each rule is selected and needed. Principles are not designed to be enforced because they are too general. They provide the reason(s) for rules and provide answers to questions about why we have them. Examples of principles previously mentioned are *Respect yourself*; *Respect each other*; and *Respect this place*. Here are some other examples:

- Be courteous.
- Be prepared.
- Treat others as they wish to be treated.
- Try your best at all times.

- Expect a safe learning environment.
- All who come in here will learn.

Effective Rules

Rules are behavioral expressions of the principles. They define clearly *what* is acceptable in the classroom and what is not. They also define *how* we are expected to behave. Rules work best when they describe specific behavior. The more specific your rules, the more you have, so we advise limiting the number of rules by starting only with the ones needed most. When possible, try expressing rules in a positive tone—for example, "Be on time" instead of "Do not be late." Some rules are hard to define in positive terms only. For example, the positive version of "Do not put down other students"—"Say only nice things about each other"—does not offer a means to express dissatisfaction. The social contract is neither the Magna Carta nor a legal brief. Get rid of words that are unnecessary or confusing. Avoid the word *try*.

The importance of specific and predictable rules is directly related to developing responsibility. The more understandable the expectations, the better the students' chances of meeting them. It is impossible to make a good choice if the system is unclear.

It is possible to overdo the specificity of a rule. Having too many rules is often felt as oppressive by "good" students and can give ideas to "bad" students they hadn't previously thought of. It is not necessary to list every objectionable swear word or put-down. When hearing inappropriate language that may not directly have a rule, the teacher is well advised to see this as an opportunity to share how an important value has been offended. Here are examples of rules that are too vague or too specific, as well as revisions that are "just right":

Too vague: "Each student must not interfere with another student's learning." (This makes a fine *principle*, but not a *rule*.)

Too specific: "Do not poke your fingers in another student's eye."

Just right: "People are not for hitting. Keep your hands and feet to yourself."

Too vague: "Do not stop others from learning."

Too specific: "Never talk when others are talking."

Just right: "Raise your hand in class discussions before making your contribution."

Figure 4.1 contains a nice balance of values and rules.

Figure 4.1
Mrs. Connor's Class Values and Rules

Value: I have a right to be happy, and to be treated with kindness in this room.

Rule: This means that no one will laugh at me, ignore me, or hurt my feelings.

Value: I have a right to be myself in this room.

Rule: This means that no one will treat me unfairly because I am fat or thin, fast or slow, boy or girl.

Value: I have a right to feel safe in this room.

Rule: This means that no one will hit me, kick me, push me, or pinch me.

Value: I have a right to hear and be heard in this room.

Rule: This means that no one will yell, scream, or shout and that my opinions and desires will be considered in any plans we make.

Value: I have a right to learn about myself in this room.

Rule: This means that I will be free to express my feelings and opinions at an appropriate time without being interrupted or punished.

Consequences

Consequences, an essential part of the social contract, can be the most difficult to develop because they may be easily confused with threats, punishments, or rewards. Sometimes the only difference is whether there is an element of choice. For example, "Bob, people are not for hitting. This is your second offense, which means two days of detention." There is no choice here. The control is completely with the teacher and the system without regard to whether the consequence will actually be effective. By contrast, a consequence could be framed as follows: "Bob, people are not for hitting. I am thinking a couple of days of detention might help you remember there are better ways to express your anger. Let me know by the end of class if you can think of an even better solution." Sometimes it is hard to see the difference between threat and choice. Notice the following examples:

"If you do not do your work now, you will miss lunch and do it then. The choice is yours!"

"Some students prefer doing their work during lunch. Would you rather do yours now or at that time?"

Notice the difference is in control. Two guidelines may help you understand the difference:

• Are the choices designed to teach better behavior, or do they rely primarily on making the student's life miserable?

• Are you making it sound like there is a choice even though you know beforehand exactly what you want the student to choose?

The following criteria for good consequences are brief because the next chapter is devoted entirely to consequences. Good consequences

• Are clear and specific,
• Have a range of alternatives,
• Are designed to teach improved behavioral choices rather than inflict misery,

• Are natural and logical when possible, and
• Are related to the rule.

Consequences also

• Preserve the student's dignity,
• Increase the internal locus of control when appropriate, and
• Increase student motivation.

Student Input

The more that students are involved in the process of developing rules and consequences, the more they feel that the plan is a part of them. Ultimately, they are more likely to follow the plan if they had a say in its development. Here are four ways to involve students.

• **Students help develop classroom values.** You can begin by asking students what kind of classroom they want to share. Here are some examples:

– We want to be heard.
– We want a chance to explain our side of the story.
– We want to be respected.

• **Students develop rules for the teacher.** Do not accept a rule or consequence for yourself that you can't live with. Most teachers can find one or two student-created rules that they can follow. Typical examples include these:

– Homework is handed back within three days of students turning it in.
– Water is the only beverage allowed in class for students and the teacher.
– Fruit and vegetables are the only foods allowed to be eaten in class. (This can lead to a lesson on what is a fruit and what is a vegetable.)
– The teacher must be on time and ready to begin teaching when the bell rings.

Using this method gives the teacher an opportunity to model the way students should respond when they are caught breaking a rule.

• **Students develop rules for themselves based on values.** The students can develop some or most of the rules that are not directly related to instruction. For example, the teacher might give students an assignment to propose three rules that are examples of "We expect a safe learning environment." Examples might include the following:

   – Do not take my stuff without asking.
   – When you see someone doing something that could be dangerous, tell an adult.
   – When angry, we can share our feelings, walk away, or ask an adult for advice.

• **Students vote on negotiable rules.** This is a nice option for younger children. Think of some (not all) rules you can let students choose by vote. For example, "You can choose where to sit one day each week." Then take a vote to determine which day each week they want it to be. Another example might have to do with choosing when students will do story time and when they will have snack time.

For young children and others with limited language skills, more structure is often useful. You might say to students:

I want to give you a chance to have some rules and consequences for me and for each other. Now, that might sound silly to some of you because usually children aren't allowed to tell grown-ups how to act. But I remember that when I was in 1st grade, I wished my teacher would say hello to me in the morning, not yell at me when I made a mistake; let me choose which of my papers to hang in the room; and, even though I was scared, call my parents when I hit someone or call someone else's parents when they hit me. How many of you would like these rules in our class?

Test for Student Comprehension

To prevent students from claiming ignorance about rules and consequences, test them on the social contract. Passing should be a perfect score. Students are permitted to take the test as many times as necessary.

Communication with Parents

Because involving parents is often a consequence of misbehavior, it is important to establish effective communication with them before problems occur. One method is to write a cover letter explaining the social contract process. Include a copy of the class social contract and a return slip for them to indicate that they have read and understood the contract. Enclosing a phone number or e-mail address for questions is also helpful. Use Parent Night at the school to explain the contract process and to share specifics, particularly as they relate to gaining parental support.

Whether or not you do a social contract, there is no substitute for contacting parents of students known to be challenging. You can contact them before school even begins. For example, you might call and say, "Ms. Rodriguez, I am going to have Enrique in my social studies class this year, and I like to call as many parents as I can before school starts. I just want to let you know a little bit about how I run the class, and I'd like to learn as much as I can from you that can help me make sure Enrique has a successful experience."

Use of Administrators

Administrators should be informed of the social contract as it is developed. This point is especially important when including administrators as part of the consequences. Many teachers can successfully gain administrators' support when they make it in the interest of administrators to support a plan. For example, if you work in a school that requires everybody to implement the same consequences in the same order, and you want to try something else, you might ask your administrator for a waiver. For example, say something like this:

> For the next grading period, I would like to try doing things a little differently with my class because I think a slight change will lead to improved decision making. Instead of giving consequences sequentially, I would like to give students the one or ones I think will work best in that situation. My goal is to see if that will allow me to send less of them to you! Can I count on your support?

It is important to show administrators how it can be in their best interests to agree with your plan.

Most administrators are eager to support reasonable actions that will require less of their time. We find that clarity between teachers and administrators around the issue of discipline helps counteract the stress associated with feelings of isolation and the perceived lack of administrative support.

Tips for Supporting the Substitute Teacher

Student eyes often light up when a substitute takes over for a day. Armed with lesson plans left by the teacher and a "good luck" wish by the administration, most substitutes are overmatched. Many spend more time dealing with behavior than with subject matter. You can make life easier for them by providing classroom guidelines. If substitutes have been informed of the social contract, the administrator can then support the substitute because they are aware of your rules and possible consequences.

If you know you are going to be absent and a substitute will be in, you might approach one or two of your more difficult students and tell them in advance. Let them know you will be calling that night to hear how things went and you expect to hear positive things. Tell them you trust they will respect the sub and help keep everyone else on task.

Example of a Social Contract

Holly Sanford, an intermediate-level art teacher, developed a social contract including monitoring and merits to improve discipline in her overcrowded art classroom. Her goals were to cut down on students moving around the classroom, talking while working, and bickering over materials. The idea was based on the children's natural inclinations to choose a leader. She sees her classes for a 13-week cycle, with each class period approximately 40 minutes long. The art room is set up with six tables that seat five students each. Figure 4.2 identifies the class process that gives students much responsibility in looking after their own and each other's behavior. Figure 4.3 identifies consequences.

Figure 4.2
Monitoring System Contract

1. Each table group will have a monitor who is in charge of getting materials, distributing them, supervising behavior according to the classroom rules, collecting materials, and cleaning up.

2. To get started, the monitor is voted on by the members of the group based on his leadership qualities, dependability, or whatever other qualities the group feels constitutes a good leader. Every two weeks, somebody new with the next-closest birthday will become the monitor.

3. All members of the group must cooperate with the monitor.

4. The monitor must fulfill the duties and responsibilities of his position.

5. After an assignment is given, nobody but the monitor may leave his seat. All questions that any group member has must first be asked of the group. If nobody knows the answer, the monitor may approach or send the student to the teacher.

Figure 4.3
Consequences for Failure to Comply
with Monitoring System Contract

1. The monitor verbally reinforces to the group that he is the person in charge.

2. The group reminds the monitor that he is the person who accepted the responsibility of being the monitor.

3. The group has a consultation with the teacher present to find out what the problem is and how to solve it. The teacher will act as a coach to help the group find a satisfactory solution.

4. Failure to resolve problems through an agreeable compromise results in group or individual consequences to be determined by the teacher.

For the Administrator

Social contracts are an integral part of the Discipline with Dignity process. As an administrator, you can be a helpful resource for teachers who wish to develop social contracts. You can help teachers by reviewing their proposed rules and consequences before they are introduced to students. Be sure their rules are tied to core school values like safety, cooperation, and respect. Your leadership in establishing school values is essential. Help clarify any rules that are not clear, and check to see if the consequences are really designed to teach improved student decision making (see Chapter 5). Advise teachers to stay away from rigidly sequencing their consequences so that they have the predictability (there will be a consequence) and flexibility (they decide which consequence is best) needed to be effective. Support and encourage them to modify consequences if things are not working in their classroom(s), but let them know you expect they will discuss changes before they are implemented.

Once the social contracts have been established, we recommend offering support by checking to see how things are going. Great administrators spend at least an hour per day in the classroom, observing teachers, giving feedback, and building relationships with students.

We think it is important to encourage your teachers to share their expectations of you and let them know what you consider to be appropriate and inappropriate demands. Clarify and discuss your role when a student breaks a rule. Let staff know a range of actions you may take if they refer students, but be equally clear in specifying that once a student is referred, the teacher has given you the discretion to make the decision you think is best.

Reassure them that your goal is always to send back a better-behaved student, and you will do your best to make that happen while realizing that tough students are not easy to change. After a student has been referred, it is advisable to wait a minimum of 15 minutes before sending the student back. Teachers really appreciate the administrator accompanying a student back to the classroom, which tends to minimize an inappropriate re-entry.

If you wish to set up a schoolwide social contract for your building, be advised that this process can be very difficult because agreement among a diverse faculty about much of anything is difficult to achieve. For example, everyone will agree that respect is important, but you are likely to hear several interpretations about whether a certain behavior crosses or doesn't cross the line. As the person in charge, you can seek consensus on rules, but do not be dependent on it. For example, when a schoolwide problem exists, such as running in the halls, be prepared to inform your staff about what you plan to do and what you expect each of them to do. Be open to other ideas, but do not allow discussion to wander and ultimately obscure your vision. If there are competing ideas that seem good, acknowledge that it may be tough for everybody to be on the same page and agree to form a diverse committee to study the issue further and make recommendations. Pick the solution that you are most comfortable with until the committee formed to study the issue is prepared to make any other recommendations.

Parents and students can also be included in developing a schoolwide social contract or in solving a schoolwide problem. If using that model, seek a cross section within each role group to be represented in the decision making. It is fine to have uniform rules, but be sure to have a wide range of consequences so you and your teachers can be "fair" without needing to treat all students the same.

A key to a school's success is that staff feel respected for their thoughts and ideas, but at the same time they understand that sometimes they will be expected to enforce rules even when they disagree. Be open to discussing another's point of view. At the same time, with proper training, all staff can learn to effectively enforce even those rules with which they personally disagree.

When a substitute teacher is assigned to a class, see that they are given a copy of the classroom social contract. If the teacher does not have a social contract, then at least provide behavioral guidelines. Also ensure that all parents understand their child's social contract. Encourage teachers to share this information during open school night or at early teacher-parent conferences. The school's PTA can also be involved in informing parents about the school rules and possible consequences.

Finally, as the school leader, it is necessary to help faculty keep in perspective the relatively *minor* role that rules and consequences play in overall discipline. For example, many problems are the result of poor student motivation, not discipline. Provide training and/or coaching in developing motivation skills and improved instructional techniques for those teachers who need it. The more students are motivated, the fewer discipline problems will exist. Remind your teachers regularly that a plan for prevention involves addressing the three Cs: connection, competence, and control.

5

Consequences

The main thing we've learned about consequences since the first edition is that a consequence is merely a vehicle to a destination. The destination is not simply for the student to be obedient, but for the student to be responsible and make the best choice. Therefore, it is most important that the consequence be designed to get a result. Although outcome is most important in deciding whether to continue using a consequence, it is essential that the consequence avoid reliance on humiliation. One of our greatest frustrations is that consequences are continuously confused with punishments.

Let's clarify: Punishments are done to others. The goal is to achieve the proper amount of misery so that the behavior will not recur. As ridiculous as it might sound, if you are late to the airport, a punishment might be to write 100 times "I won't be late to the airport" or to post your name on the monitor with a check mark next to it. A punishment makes it easy to blame the messenger and to harbor resentment.

Consequences are what we do to ourselves. They are the results of our choices. The goal is to teach improved decision making in the absence of authority. If you are late to the airport, the consequence is you miss your flight. A consequence helps us learn to make better choices. It gets us to look inside and take responsibility so we can fix our mistake.

Our definition suggests that a consequence cannot really be predetermined because it is the effect, result, or outcome of something else. If that something hasn't happened yet, then how can we know the outcome? For example, a golfer goes to the driving range and works on his swing for three hours. We can guess that the consequence will be improvement in his golf game. But what if he practices incorrectly for three hours? Maybe he'll actually get worse. Either way, we do not know until he gets out on the course. This is why it is fine to have a range of possible consequences, but we better leave room for one not on the list.

Punishments are very different. They are based on the principle of deterrence. During 18th-century England, pickpockets were publicly hanged in front of large crowds to deter future pickpocketing. The spectators frequently had their pockets picked during the hangings by those not deterred.

Most teachers and administrators we work with use the words *consequence* and *punishment* interchangeably. Difficult students need consequences. They need to see that their behavior has repercussions. It is impossible to punish most difficult students more than life already has.

Finally, it is so important to realize that most times, effective discipline is about managing behavior without needing a consequence. For example, having effective cues can sometimes replace the need for a consequence. We recently met a teacher who was fed up with the lesson-killing questions "Can I get a drink?" and "Can I go to the bathroom?" So this teacher created a cue. When Sally raised her hand with the index finger up in the air, it meant "bathroom." When the pinky was raised, it meant "drink." When a full fist was raised it meant "question about the lesson." This allowed the teacher to know what the student was going to ask before she asked it.

Students Learn More When They Have a Say in Their Consequence

Many of us are afraid to involve our students in the process of developing consequences. At the time of the first edition of this book, we were, too. We advocated having students create values and rules, but not consequences. We have changed. Students need to have a say in all three. Starting with values as a guide, rules need to be specific, and consequences need to make sense. Here is an example of a student creating his or her own consequence:

Student: I do not want to stay after school to develop a behavior plan with you.
Teacher: You know what? I don't care if you stay, either. In fact, why don't you come up with a consequence that will work better? And if you do not come up with something, then I guess I'll see you after school.

Remember, the outcome of the consequence is what we care about. It is not the specific consequence that matters most.

How We Do It Is More Important Than What We Do

The way we implement a consequence is more important than the consequence itself. It is best to put yourself at the receiving end of a consequence and ask yourself whether your dignity would be preserved or attacked. Consequences are best delivered calmly, privately, and with the utmost dignity.

Stop Sequencing Specific Consequences

In almost every school and classroom we visit, teachers post rules and consequences. Almost always the consequences or punishments are numbered and in order. We call these *sequenced consequences*. They look something like this:

First offense: Warning

Second offense: Phone call home

Third offense: Detention

Fourth offense: In-school suspension

Fifth offense: Out-of-school suspension

Does this look familiar? If it does, instead of having sequenced consequences, tell your students, "These are the consequences when you break a rule. One of these will happen, but there is no predetermined order. Either you or I will pick the most appropriate one, based on what will help you the most."

Sequencing consequences forces us to do things that might not work. For some children, a phone call home is like a "get out of jail free card" because their parents are never there. Others love detention because it allows them to stay after school in a safe, structured environment. Consequences should be structured to be both *predictable* and *flexible*.

Like a good doctor treating each patient's unique symptoms to heal that person, a teacher should always do what is right for each student to teach better behavior. Be very clear with your class that you will use the consequence that best fits each individual situation.

Be Fair, Not Necessarily Equal

Teaching better behavior requires giving each student what she needs, can understand, and can do. Many times, abilities and circumstances vary as do the personalities of our students. One student may never do homework, whereas another misses an assignment because her father got sick and was taken to the hospital. Although we know that different consequences are sometimes necessary even though students may have violated the same rule, the teacher will often hear complaints of being unfair.

It is extremely important to explain and teach your students that "fair and equal" can but do not have to mean the same thing (Mendler, Curwin, & Mendler, 2008). This is best done before any issue related to discipline occurs, although it is never too late. In school, the word *fair* should be defined as "Each student gets what he or she needs to be *successful* and act in a more *responsible* way." Let your students know that your goal each day is for each student to get better at your subject today than he was yesterday—not necessarily better than everybody else but better than himself. Furthermore, let students know that if they break a rule, you will do whatever you believe is best to help each student make a better choice. Therefore, consequences will not always be the same for each student.

When students complain about a consequence, invite another alternative, but do not discuss the other student. It sounds like this:

Violet: I can't believe you are making me stay after school and you are calling Jen's mom. That's not fair!

Teacher: Violet, what's the problem with the consequence I gave you?

Violet: But Jen got . . . .

Teacher (cutting Violet off): I know what Jen got, and I'm not here to talk to you about her. What's the problem with what I did for you?

Violet: But Jen did the same . . . .

Teacher: Violet, when you are ready to talk about what could work better for you, I will be glad to listen.

Many teachers incorrectly think they have to justify what they are doing with one student to the entire class. You must let your students know "I will not talk about someone else to you, nor will I talk about you to someone else."

In framing the difference between *fair* and *equal*, consider the following examples to share with your students:

• Is it fair to expect a student in a wheelchair to shower after physical education class without a special needs shower facility?

• Is it fair to ask hearing-impaired students to watch an uncaptioned video and take a test on it?

• Is it fair to give the same Spanish test to a native speaker and a student who has never spoken it before class?

Ask your students to think of other examples of fair not necessarily meaning equal in life. Here are some starters:

• In baseball, closers are paid a lot of money to pitch one inning and shortstops have to play nine. Often the pitcher even makes more money (which is certainly not equal but is fair).
• Different-aged children have different chores at home (which is fair but not equal).
• Some children wear glasses and others do not (which also is fair but not equal).

After explaining and teaching the difference between these two words, conclude by saying something like this:

> I need to let you know that I will do my best to be fair to each and every one of you in this room, which means Stefan and Bobby might get different consequences if I think they need different things to not make the same mistake. If you ever think there is a better consequence for you than the one I chose, let me know what you think it is, and I will be happy to listen, but please do not complain about what happened to someone else.

If students think they have a better way to improve their behavior, encourage them to express their ideas. This can be an important component in teaching responsibility. For example:

Student: I do not think that I should have to stay after school today, because that consequence is not best for me!
Teacher: OK, why not?
Student: Because a behavior plan will not get me to change my behavior. But if you move my seat away from those other two girls, I promise I'll behave.
Teacher: Sounds good. I'll move your seat tomorrow. And starting tomorrow I trust you will behave yourself in this class! By the way, just in case this doesn't work, what other consequence(s) do you think would be fair?

Finally, some teachers might find it overwhelming to give each student what that child needs all the time. Remember, fair and equal can mean the same thing. They just do not have to. In many instances, the same consequence might work for several students. By implementing this policy, you are saying you reserve the right to be equal but promise to be fair!

Consistency for Caring, Predictability for Consequences

When students perceive consequences as random, they begin to doubt that they can influence their future. Many ask us how we're being consistent if we aren't always giving the same consequences. We believe the best definition of *consistent* is *always* caring about each of your students. And caring means doing what will best help each student be successful and become more responsible. Students will not make good choices if they cannot anticipate what the results of those choices will be. When a teacher accepts minor infractions while slowly reaching a breaking point, and then lashes out at one student while others are also violating the rule, students see the classroom as a game of musical chairs.

Besides Teaching Improved Decision Making, What Else Should Consequences Do?

Specific and predictable consequences serve several purposes besides teaching better decision making.

• **Preserve dignity.** As stated earlier, be sure to place yourself at the receiving end of a consequence and ask whether a "consequence" would preserve or attack your dignity (e.g., you show up late to a faculty meeting, and the principal writes your name on the board).

• **Seek to increase responsibility.** Good consequences help students understand what is within their control to change, what is beyond their control, and how to deal with what they cannot change without feeling helpless.

• **Increase student motivation.** Punishments decrease motivation because they create strong negative feelings that make learning difficult or impossible. They may change behavior for the short term. But we are interested in keeping students motivated to learn over the long haul. When an intervention for misbehavior leaves the child with a negative attitude for a long time, that student's desire to learn diminishes. Some students become so angered by an embarrassing or threatening teacher that they give up on that class for the entire school year. When a student is caught breaking a rule, we do not expect him to immediately return to his schoolwork full of enthusiasm and joy. We do, however, expect him to focus on how he can improve the situation and not hold resentment to the point of danger.

Four Types of Consequences

We have divided consequences into four types:

• Generic—they can be connected to any rule.
• Conventional—conventional punishments can be changed into effective consequences.
• Educational—they are specifically designed to teach new behaviors.
• Natural/logical—they are the result of students' choices.

Generic Consequences

There are four types of generic consequences that can be tied to any rule.

REMINDER OR WARNING OF RULE

For example, "Sholanda, we raise our hands before speaking. This is your reminder. I trust you will not need to be reminded again. Thanks for following the rule." When stated more firmly, this statement becomes a warning.

AN ACTION PLAN FOR IMPROVING BEHAVIOR

For example, "Caleb, being out of your seat bothering Ava is not OK. I want you to come up with a plan for how you are going to stop bothering her. If you can't come up with a plan on your own, I will help you. But I trust you can. I look forward to seeing it soon."

Stay away from simply having students fill out an action plan form like this:

Answer the three following questions:

1. What did I do?
2. What should I do?
3. What will I do?

Most will fill it out with no real commitment to change.

1. What did I do? FIGHT
2. What should I do? NOT FIGHT
3. What will I do? I WON'T FIGHT

Here is an example of working with a student to help build responsibility by developing a plan:

Teacher: Will you have your homework tomorrow?
Student: Yeah, I think so.
Teacher (feeling skeptical): When will you start?
Student: After dinner.
Teacher: What time?
Student: At 7 p.m.
Teacher: How long will you spend?
Student: Whenever.
Teacher: Can you guess a number?
Student: Twenty minutes.

Teacher: Where will you do it?

Student: In my room.

Teacher: With or without TV?

Student: Without.

Teacher: And if someone calls?

Student: I'll call back later.

Teacher: So you'll have your homework tomorrow?

Student: Yeah.

Teacher: That's great, but in case you do not, what do you think are fair consequences?

In script, this dialogue sounds like an interrogation; but in conversation, it is less stringent, and it works. The contingency questions lead to commitment. Now the teacher and student can write it down to have a record, but the plan is not the paper. The plan is the steps the student has agreed to take. Once the interaction is complete, a good, strong handshake seals the deal. Without some kind of commitment, there is little chance of the plan working.

HELPING OTHERS

Perhaps the best consequence we know is community service by helping another student. Typically the student being helped is younger or has a disability. Here are some helping opportunities:

- Tutoring
- Being a field trip partner
- Developing an action plan to solve a problem with the target student
- Being a bodyguard to student who is being bullied or teased
- Monitoring the playground or cafeteria
- Reading stories to younger children

The academic skill of the helper is unimportant. The goal is to let the student give back to the community because she took something by behaving inappropriately. We love this consequence because along with restitution, it is also a powerful healing process for children who have been hurt by factors in their life they can't control. Here are three powerful life examples of how helping others can play a significant role in healing:

• Soldiers returning from war with lost limbs helping other returning soldiers with a similar condition learn to walk

• Hurricane victims who have lost everything helping others rebuild their homes

• Cancer survivors helping new cancer patients deal with the emotional stress of discovering they have cancer

HUMOROUS CONSEQUENCES

Humor can often be utilized to make a point. We know a teacher who makes up lyrics to the song "Since You've Been Gone" and sings this as students arrive late or after an unexcused absence. For example (in song), "Sally, nice to see you. (Singing) Since you've been gone, we have covered the battle of Gettysburg." The teacher who does this shared that rarely do students come late because they do not want to be serenaded.

Conventional Consequences

Conventional consequences include detention, phone calls home, and referrals to another staff person's office.

DETENTION

A wise woman once said, "Never send your children to bed when they are bad; send them to bed when they are good." Her point was that if bed is a punishment, then children won't want to go. Never make something you want students to like a punishment. The same is true for detention (or staying after school). What message do we send about school if we make them stay longer when misbehaving? Instead, make time after school relevant to improving the behavior that convinced you to detain them.

Here are three principles for detaining children:

• The teacher who assigns the detention stays with the student and deals with why the student is there.

• The time is used to discuss, practice, or teach new skills.

• No set time (e.g., three hours). When the goal is met, the detention is over.

PHONE CALLS HOME

Calls home work best when the call is to ask for a suggestion about how the parent might help solve a problem. Dumping a problem on a parent rarely results in a positive outcome. Try something like this:

Teacher: Hello, Mrs. Green. This is Mrs. Singe. Ahmad got in a fight today, and I thought if we work together, we can help teach him a better way to solve his problems. I'd really like to hear what you think and how I can help.

REFERRALS TO OFFICE

Referrals work best when they are reserved for serious problems that require an administrator. Our guideline is "Does the rule violation break the law?" Is it an assault, harassment, drug sale, or sexual misbehavior? The problem with referrals is that the one who solves the problem is the one who earns the student's respect. Teachers who refer on a regular basis lose the confidence and respect of all students, not only those referred. Referrals often lead to a worsening of behavior.

Here's how to make referrals effective as consequences:

• For times when you need a break from a student—and these do happen—send the student to another teacher, social worker, or counselor.

• Let the student choose when to come back. For example, "Kelly, we are headed for a major disagreement. Please take a break in Mrs. Prague's class and come back when you are ready to learn. Please do not be too long. This lesson is too important for you to miss."

• With the free time the administrator gains with fewer referrals, she can become more visible in the school by greeting students at the front door in the morning, in the cafeteria, or other places in the building. She can devote more of her time to dealing with the more serious offenses.

Educational Consequences

When students break a rule, do not assume they know better. Just as good academic instruction includes explanation, demonstration, practice, repetition, and evaluation, so, too, should these components be highlighted when teaching better behavior. Whether in class, the hallway, or anywhere else in the building, it is our responsibility to correct inappropriate behavior and then teach a better way. We have found the following instruction to be highly effective with most students:

1. Identify the problem behavior with the student and ask the student whether he thinks it would be OK to keep doing the same thing?

2. If the student does not understand that his behavior was wrong, explain why it was.

3. Following your explanation, ask the student to explain what was wrong in his own words.

4. Re-create the situation that led to trouble as near as possible and demonstrate through role play at least one appropriate way of handling the situation. It is usually best to have the student provoke you in the same way that he was provoked that led to his problem behavior. Then demonstrate a better response.

5. Ask the student to practice the response you used or another that might be equally effective without leading to trouble.

6. Switch roles and tell the student that you are going to try to provoke him in the same way that led to trouble and you want him to practice using what was just rehearsed.

7. Repeat a few times to polish.

8. Evaluate and adjust as needed. If you notice the student using the strategy effectively, point it out. Sometimes, the strategy will need to be practiced more or modified so that the student can use it naturally.

Natural/Logical Consequences

Natural or logical consequences (Driekers, 1964) are the direct result of our choices. If we don't wear a coat on a cold day, the consequence is that we feel cold. Here are a few examples of natural/logical consequences in school:

• If a student messes up a bathroom, a logical consequence is for that student to clean it up.

• If a student hurts another student, a logical consequence is for the offending student to do something nice for the hurt student or to do something constructive for the school.

• If a student comes to class late, she stays late.

Other Ways to Develop Effective Consequences

Colleagues at school as well as parents can be additional sources of ideas for consequences.

Collect from Others

Do not hesitate to collect effective consequences from other teachers and administrators. Often teachers feel that they must do everything for themselves when it comes to discipline, although they exchange subject-matter ideas more freely. One or two good consequences from each teacher can provide 50 to 100 total.

Invite Parent Suggestions

Parents often know what is best for their child. Allow them to have a say. If a parent says, "I do not like the consequence you gave my son!" a response might be "I thought my consequence would help your child. You know her better than I do. Do you have better ideas for how to make that happen? Because if you do, I'd be glad to hear them."

Evaluating Consequences

In deciding whether a consequence is effective, it is best to implement it as many as five times or for a trial period of three weeks. If you notice positive changes interspersed with the same old poor behavior during this time, consider the consequence effective. Although there are wonderful moments when a break-through to better behavior occurs, better behavior rarely happens right away.

Change is usually a gradual process, with people needing to visit their old behaviors as they acquire new ones. A realistic goal is for a consequence to help a student gradually replace the poor behavior with a better one.

Obstacles to Effective Consequences

A few systemic obstacles can diminish the effectiveness of our consequences. The teacher may not be comfortable with a consequence because it does not mesh with her style. Sometimes schools require teachers to implement consequences that do not fit with the individual teacher. To avoid this situation, it is best to be proactive and propose an alternative for your classroom that you think will work better. Most administrators are willing to accept a well-conceived alternative for at least a trial period.

Another obstacle is that the rule violation occurs at an inconvenient place or time. It may be in a part of the room physically distant from the teacher or at a time when the teacher is involved with other students. It can seem like a lot of work to interrupt a lesson and quietly go over to a student who has just broken a rule. To avoid having to do so, it is important to tell your class early in the school year:

> I need to let you all know there may be times that some of you will say or do inappropriate things this year. Believe me, it happens every year. I just want to let you know that I won't always stop the lesson to deal with that person. Some of you might even wonder what I'm going to do about it. Trust me, I do not ignore misbehavior, but I also do not believe in stopping a lesson or in embarrassing any of you. At the proper time, I'll deal with it. But it will be dealt with when I see fit. Is there anything you don't understand about this?

Now you can stop the lesson if the student needs to be dealt with, or you can continue teaching if you feel teaching is more important in that moment.

A Case Study

A school where we recently consulted was experiencing considerable problems in managing the behavior of its students in the cafeteria. The staff's plan for solving this problem illustrates the use of consequences as well as other factors that make for an effective social contract.

A discipline committee at this midsized, lower-middle-class elementary school worked on developing a schoolwide social contract based on the principles of Discipline with Dignity. The committee was composed of two students, one administrator, two teachers, and two parents. They identified student cafeteria behavior as the schoolwide discipline problem that required attention. As a result of their work, the following plan was developed:

Cafeteria Values

1. Eating should be pleasant and comfortable.
2. The cafeteria should be safe.

Cafeteria Rules

1. Students will raise their hands and are expected to receive the permission of cafeteria supervisors before they may leave their seats.
2. The cafeteria is a place to whisper, not to scream, whistle, or yell.
3. Food is for eating, not for throwing.
4. Fighting is not permitted under any conditions or for any reason.
5. Each class will have an assigned table in the cafeteria. Students are to clean their area after they have finished eating.
6. Students are to walk in the cafeteria, not run.
7. Students may go through the lunch line only once—with their class.

Consequence Options

• Students receive a warning.
• A letter is sent home from the principal to the student's parents.
• A parent-teacher-principal-student meeting is held to come up with a plan for improved decision making.
• Student eats at a separate table, maybe even by him- or herself.
• Students stay after school to help the janitor clean the cafeteria.
• Student helps serve in the cafeteria.
• Other.

Before this plan could be implemented, all teachers were expected to have a thorough discussion with their classes. Following this discussion, teachers administered a test for comprehension to guarantee that each student knew the rules and the possible consequences if the rules were broken.

The lists of values, rules, and possible consequences were posted in the cafeteria and each classroom. They were also mailed to parents. Although this school's discipline problems have not been completely eliminated, cafeteria behavior is much improved. The success of this program can be attributed to the specificity of the rules and possible consequences, along with schoolwide support for the program and clear guidelines for the teachers, cafeteria supervisors, and students. Each teacher thoroughly discussed the contract with the class, administered and scored a uniform test for comprehension, posted the Cafeteria Contract in the classroom, monitored the records kept by cafeteria supervisors, and consistently implemented consequences they thought to be effective. The cafeteria supervisors kept accurate records of student violators and shared this information with teachers.

For the Administrator

It is important to recognize that a teacher's referral is usually an expression of frustration. You must be a good active listener for teachers and students, even when receiving referrals that you believe are unwarranted. We have found that many teachers want their administrator to be "tough" with students when they are referred to your office. You loom as an alternative for many who would really like to open their window and drop the student from the third floor. Be sure to help the student come up with a plan for how he is going to behave upon returning. It is then helpful to walk the student back to class so that the teacher knows you spent some time with the student.

Great administrators view themselves as teachers first. They should always be there to help the referred student improve her behavior and maybe the teacher's as well. When students are referred, it is important to encourage the teacher and student to solve their own problems. Act as a facilitator to help each party solve the problem (preferably together). Although you can remain open to having teachers refer students to you, impress upon your staff that each time they send a student to somebody else, they are disempowering themselves. They are really telling the student that they are unable to handle things, which is obviously not a good message to send to that student or to others in the class. It can be helpful to devote some staff time to role-playing various incidents that often lead to referral while demonstrating another way to handle the behavior in the classroom.

Reducing student referrals frees your time. Use that time to become more visible in the school. Greet students at the main entrance. Go into the library. Be in the corridors. Most important, visit every classroom at least once a week so students and teachers know that you are active and available.

Have a wide range of consequences, but let the teachers decide which is best for a given situation. If you have a school or district policy that requires certain actions, be open to a well-conceived alternative from your teachers that might work better. See if you can find a way to allow the alternative to flourish for a trial period while evaluating its effectiveness.

Although it is always appropriate to treat all with respect and dignity, fairness in your interactions with staff means helping each be as successful with students as possible. Therefore, you will not always treat everyone exactly the same way. If you think a student is a better fit with one teacher than with another, and placing that student will give the teacher more students than others, it is sometimes necessary to make that decision anyway. Explain your reasoning to the receiving teacher by highlighting her strengths rather than the limitations of others.

If you get a comparative complaint from a teacher (e.g., "I have 28 students, but he has 25), the response needs to be "I know what he has, and you have more because you are able to handle those students, in my mind. I'm not here to discuss him, but let's talk about what you need to make your situation work." This approach will greatly reduce the complaining and gossiping among your faculty and staff.

6

Taking Action

When we first wrote *Discipline with Dignity*, we believed that once consequences were established, all the teacher had to do was implement them in an effective way, and the problem would be solved. We now realize how much more complicated this process is. Many factors influence the effectiveness of an intervention, including these:

- The teacher's attitude toward rule violations
- The consistency of enforcement
- The ability of the teacher to choose the best consequence
- The ability of students to develop their own consequences
- The style of consequence implementation
- What happens when more than one student is acting out
- What the teacher does when a student refuses to accept a consequence.

There are many times when consequences are not the best interventions. Building relationships, developing trust, and simply listening are often very helpful interventions that do not involve active consequence implementation. We mentioned the difference between obedience and responsibility in Chapter 1. Let's examine how obedience and responsibility affect specific actions when a rule is broken.

Punishment and Reward as Interventions

The two major categories of obedience interventions are *punishment* and *reward.*

Let's look first at punishment. Have you ever gotten a speeding ticket? If so, did you say, "Great, now I'll be a better driver!" or "Darn, I should have seen the cop!" The reason you got a ticket is because you got caught. Students who have strong positive social values are reminded by punishment that they did wrong. Punishment is, therefore, most helpful for the best students. However, students who continually break rules have not developed positive social values and make bad choices most of the time. They learn from punishment "not to get caught." The more a student is punished, the less it affects him because he grows accustomed to it.

Now let's look more closely at rewards as an intervention. Despite all of the research and strong repudiation of rewards in the last decade, rewards are a major component in even more programs than before. We now have color-coded systems; point accumulation systems; best student of the day, week, and month systems; and a host of other reward-based methods designed to increase the level of student obedience. As we (the authors) fervently discussed this topic among ourselves, we found many differences based more on word definitions than what is best for children. The word *reward* has many different meanings and interpretations.

The classic definition of a reward-based intervention is to give a student something good, in either words (praise) or materials, so he will repeat a desired behavior. Other definitions include appreciation, encouragement, support, and acknowledgment. We firmly believe that appreciation, encouragement, support, and noticing good work are more helpful than classic rewards for a positive learning environment. They offer feedback and are expressions of feelings. Classic rewards are manipulations to get something in return. For example, many teachers believe in "catching a student being good," but there is great variation of what to do with the student when she's been caught. With all this lack of clarity, it is hard for a teacher to know what is being referred to when the word *reward* is used and how to use rewards as an intervention. Here's a guide:

• **Classic rewards.** We do not believe classic rewards have much value with most children as a behavioral intervention. However, for students without much hope for independent living, getting and holding a job, or getting married and having a family due to severe emotional, behavioral, or cognitive disability, rewards cannot hurt and can have significant value in teaching very basic skills. Furthermore, when control is the primary goal, as it sometimes can be when working with students who have severe behavior problems, reward-based systems can be helpful because they can lead to improved student behavior as long as the student values the reward. Unfortunately, rarely is there carryover when the reward is no longer given. When one of the authors was teaching 7th grade and ran out of stickers, students went ballistic. "Where's my sticker?" they cried. They were actually addicted to them and refused to work without them. What was thought to be a useful motivational tool was actually a crippling device that stopped learning.

• **Choice.** Because choice is a major factor in developing responsibility, the more students can choose the behaviors to be rewarded, as well as the reward, the more useful the reward becomes. A good example is giving yourself an extra hour of a treasured activity for losing a specific amount of weight.

• **Expectation.** If students are told in advance they will get something for being good (a form of bribery) or come to expect a reward even if it hasn't been spelled out before, then there is more of a chance the resultant expected behavior will not be internalized. In general, if the teacher's goal of giving something to the student is an expected behavior change, then it is manipulative and eventually will stop working once students stop valuing the reward. This usually happens quickly. If the goal is to express a feeling, share an appreciation, or get a student to recognize her improvement, then it can be helpful. Therefore, rewards work best when given occasionally or unexpectedly, as a gesture of appreciation.

• **Goal of the student.** If the student changes his behavior simply to get something, the reward is teaching a negative value. Do you hear students asking, "What do I get?" When the student sees a reward as a thank-you for doing the right thing rather than entitlement for good behavior, it has more of a positive impact.

Three Important Alternatives to Punishments and Rewards

If we wish to stop or greatly reduce the use of classic rewards and punishments, the following three options can help.

Use Challenge Rather Than Threat or Reward

Change is hard. Even when we want to change something about ourselves, change is hard. So how hard is it to change a child who does not want to change? It is almost impossible. We can get surface change or the appearance of change, but nothing real or substantial. The child might show enough change to avoid punishment or to get a reward, but not enough to sustain significant new behavior. Good coaches know that challenge works better than threat. When we challenge students rather than threaten them, they change because they want to. Here's a real classroom example.

Rodney, a resistant 9th grade student, refused to sit down. His teacher said, "Rodney, sit down."

Rodney: I'm not going to, and you can't make me.

Teacher: You are right. I can't make you, and I am not sure I want to, either. It takes a lot of courage to do something after saying you won't. But do not worry, not every student is brave.

Rodney thought for a moment and sat down. A few minutes later, the teacher told him privately, "I know that was hard for you, but I really appreciate it."

Model What You Want Students to Do Differently

Role modeling is very important in the moral development of children. The two most important role models in a child's life are usually her parents and teachers. To see how role modeling works in a real school situation, imagine the following event:

Two students, the age you work with, are in the cafeteria. One says to the other, "You are stupid and ugly; everyone hates you, especially me. Why don't you leave?"

What advice would you have for the victim?

- Walk away.
- Say, "I do not like that—please stop."
- Ignore it.
- Other (be specific).

Now ask yourself if that student said the same things to you, would you

- Walk away?
- Say, "I do not like that—please stop"?
- Ignore it?
- Other (be specific)?

We are most effective when we model things we tell children to do for two reasons. First, no child can do what he has never seen. We lose credibility with children who see us behave differently than we tell them to do.

Teach Students How to Change

Imagine that at the beginning of this book we told you to have three basics for running your class:

- Have students follow all rules.
- Have them behave appropriately at all times.
- Have them work at their highest capacity at all times.

Now, what question would you ask? Answer: *How?!*

All of the rewards and punishments in the world will not help a child do something that he does not know how to do. Only teaching him how will solve the problem. A difficulty for many who have mastered a task is explaining what to do and how to do it to someone else. But that is what teachers are supposed to do. Think of how hard it is to learn to drive a car with manual transmission. When your dad said, "Let out the clutch while easing on the gas," you asked, "How?" Your dad thought he *was* saying "how," but he was really saying "what." You needed to see him do it and then practice doing it many times yourself before mastering it.

If a student is approached just before the beginning of class by a friend who says, "I really have to talk to you," the student might be late for class. The problem is not irresponsibility but lack of the skill of disengagement. The best solution is to teach the child a way to handle the situation without letting the friend down and still getting to class on time (e.g., "I'd love to help now, but I must to get to class. I'm free next period"). Teaching and reinforcing the skill works better than rewarding or punishing.

The Importance of Teacher Attitude

Most misbehavior is not directed at the teacher. When teachers personalize rule violations, they may fight unnecessary battles and escalate a simple rule violation into a major confrontation. It is not necessary to make the rule violator an example for the rest of the class. Teachers certainly have a right to teach, and all students have the right to learn, but children also have a right to make mistakes and to behave in ways that are developmentally appropriate for them. Sometimes the demand for children to behave in a certain way is biologically and emotionally unnatural. When a rule is broken, interpret the incident as an opportunity for that child to see the effects of her behavior so she can begin to learn a better way. Look at the following example:

Student: You are the worst, stupidest, meanest teacher in the world!!

Teacher: Wow, you are so angry. When you calm down, I hope you will tell me how I can be better. It is hard to hear you when you call me those names.

Two Powerful Interventions: Stabilization and Reframing

Stabilization

Emergency room doctors, police officers, firefighters, and soldiers all know that it is dangerous to go forward in unstable situations. Before things can be made better, they must stop getting worse. In the emergency room, doctors stop the bleeding before they begin the healing process. Most patients are then treated for improvement once they are stable.

The same is true in the classroom. When students misbehave, teachers must first stabilize things to avoid confrontation, escalation, and in general making matters worse. A student confronts a teacher in front of the entire class by saying, "This class really sucks." The teacher responds, "Are you telling me how you really feel?" The student says strongly, "Yes." The teacher then replies, "I always appreciate honesty. Thank you for the courage to tell the truth. Let's sit down together and find a way to improve things for both of us. When are you available?" Stabilizing involves reducing anger, avoiding power struggles, and lowering the noise that can increase hostility to the point where interventions cannot work.

Reframing

Reframing is the skill of understanding a situation in a way that gives us the best chance for a positive outcome (Molnar & Linquist, 1990). It is not about making excuses for or ignoring behavior. How we behave will depend on whether we see a student as strong-willed or stubborn. Which of the following responses do you think would work better as a reaction to defiance?

1. "I love the way you never give up. You never quit. Most students your age stop the minute it gets difficult, but not you. You have the guts to keep fighting. But in this case I think it's time to realize that it's not going to work out. I think it's time to stop."

2. "You are so stubborn. When are you going to listen to me?"

We were teaching a summer school weekend course for teachers at St. Joseph's University in Philadelphia. One weekend a woman came to the course with a new baby who needed a lot of attention—feeding, rocking, and comforting. Sometimes the baby bothered other participants, and the student missed about half the class attending to the child. Which was she?

• An irresponsible student who thought more of her needs than the class.

• A responsible student who knew that she would miss a lot of the class but came anyway because she cared about her own students and wanted to learn as much as she could to improve her teaching.

As you can see, the instructor's perception of the student's behavior can dramatically influence a response. We cannot always make students do what we want, but we can determine how we see what they do.

EXAMPLES OF REFRAMING

Notice in these examples that the teacher is getting the student to want to change, modeling how to deal with a conflict, and teaching a new response.

• A 3rd grader says to her teacher, "I'm not taking a time-out, and you can't make me." Reframing the student's "arrogance" to "honesty said in a bad way," the teacher waits a moment, takes a deep breath to calm herself, and privately says, "I'm very glad you were honest with me when you told me that you didn't want a time-out. But the way you said it was more appropriate for someone who might hurt you. If your grandmother asked you to do something and you didn't want to do it, what would you say and how would you say it?"

• Recall the stabilization example cited earlier in which a student confronts a teacher in front of the entire class and says, "This class really sucks." The teacher reframes the student's arrogance into "being angry and not knowing or using an appropriate way to express it." He waits a few minutes, approaches the student privately, and says calmly, "I can see how angry you were when you said that to me in front of the class. I can appreciate that. But I can't hear you when you talk like that. Could you hear me if I said that to you in front of your friends? Let me show you a better way to express your feelings to me."

Eight Ideas for Taking Action Effectively

Once a rule is broken or an inappropriate behavior is observed, eight important ideas will help convert the situation into a growth experience for you and your students.

• **How we implement a consequence is often more important in determining its effectiveness than the consequence itself.** This applies the principle of *what* versus *how*. Notice the difference in how the consequence of time-out is implemented:

1. "You are not allowed to talk to me that way. Take a time-out for 10 minutes and think about what you did. Never do that again."
2. "I'm offended by what you said. It hurt my feelings. Take a time-out and come back when you are ready to talk respectfully to me. Please do not take too long."

How we communicate nonverbally is even more powerful than our words. In the classroom, this means that an assertive gait and gestures communicate confidence, control, and positive feelings of esteem. When we carry ourselves in an assertive manner, we are telling our students that we feel good about who we are and what we do.

• **Simply state the rule and consequence, and offer the value the rule is based on.** By remembering that the student who broke the rule was not out to get you, you will minimize your need to punish. Avoid long explanations, lecturing, scolding, retaliating, or making the student feel guilty. These approaches only escalate the problem by generating angry and hostile feelings in your students. All that is usually necessary is to respectfully state the rule and the consequence. For example: "Jose, I see that you have something important to say. Right now it's not your turn. I'll see that you get a turn in a few minutes. Please be silent until then."

We often forget to be concise because we want to make sure our students have the same understanding we do. If the student needs help following the rules, provide instruction after school or when you both have time, and demonstrate how to follow them. Then have the student practice the correct behavior.

• **Use the power of proximity.** Be as physically close to the student as possible when you implement a consequence without violating personal space. The closer you are to a student when you calmly implement the consequence, the more effective you will be. We recommend that for middle and senior high school students, you calmly go as close as conversation distance, which is about an arm's length away, then move one step closer. This is usually a safe yet powerful distance for delivering your message, although sometimes cultural or emotional issues might determine a different comfort zone. In all cases, good teacher judgment is required because we are not interested in overwhelming the student; rather, we want to convey respect in an assertive manner. With younger children, you can usually move even closer as you state the rule and consequence. It is also a good idea to put your hands in your pocket so you appear less threatening.

• **Make direct eye contact when you deliver a consequence.** As you repeat the rule and consequence, look directly at the student and capture her eyes with yours. A gentle hand on the shoulder is an effective adjunct to eye contact. After you have finished delivering your message, maintain eye contact for a second or two and then move away. Continue with your lesson. Be aware, however, that some cultures view eye contact as a sign of disrespect. In some Native American, Asian, and European cultures, for example, children do not look adults in the eye. Some students for emotional reasons cannot handle eye contact. It is far more effective in these cases to avoid insisting on eye contact compliance.

• **Use a soft yet firm tone of voice.** Be sure your comments are clear and slowly paced to make a strong impact. With practice, you can deliver a message so that only the student hears it. Doing so ensures privacy and maintains the dignity of the student.

• **Do not embarrass the student in front of peers.** It is important to avoid power struggles that emerge when a student needs to save face with peers. Public displays of consequence implementation embarrass the student and often make it difficult for the student to hear the message. Although avoiding a public conflict is sometimes impossible, privacy in implementing consequences is a helpful way for all to save face. Remember, your goal is to keep teaching, and you need to minimize words or gestures to get the message across without worsening the situation. Shielding the rule breaker from public embarrassment will give all of the other students in class the message that their right to privacy will be maintained, that their integrity will be preserved, and that they are expected to behave in class.

• **Be firm and anger-free when correcting behavior.** We have seen teachers who give consequences as if they are sorry that they have to give them. These teachers are telling their students that they fear them, and the students learn quickly that this teacher is easily intimidated. Often this kind of delivery ends with the teacher pleading with the student to stop or a consequence will be delivered later. For example: "Oh, Matilda, please stop hitting Gwen. Uh, OK? Please? If you do not, then I'm going to have to call your mother, and I do not really want to do that. So will you stop?"

On the other hand, an overly aggressive delivery can create hostility, resentment, and fear. These are not emotions that lend themselves to setting up a growth-producing interchange. Imagine a teacher pointing his index finger at a student and shouting in a loud voice, "Chou, you listen, pal! Knock it off this second, or maybe you would prefer an afternoon's worth of detention!"

We find that the most effective delivery is animated but devoid of either fear or hostility from the teacher. It is delivered assertively. Words are spoken slowly, and the teacher presents herself with assurance and confidence. The teacher demonstrates seriousness, caring, and support to the student. For example: "Nwali, we use words like 'Please stop' when we are mad, not fists."

• **Do not accept excuses, but keep the door open to another solution.** If you are sure that the rule was broken, implement the consequence as directly and expeditiously as possible. If students want to explain or argue, invite them to see you later and give them an opportunity to come up with something better if they can.

Teacher: Ashley, in this class we respect each other's property. Please leave Monica's backpack alone. Your consequence is to help Monica put her things together in a neat way.

Ashley: But it wasn't my fault; Monica started it.

Teacher: Ashley, I am sure you had your reasons, but in this class we respect each other's property. (Teacher moves away.) Now class, who can tell me what the square root of 16 is?

If the student denies or tries to bargain, acknowledge that the student might have another view and invite the student to see you later if she wishes. For example: "I'll be happy to see you after class if you have a better idea about how to fix the problem."

Avoiding Power Struggles

One of the most troublesome problems that teachers face is the power struggle. The typical power struggle occurs when the teacher makes a request and a student refuses to comply. The cycle continues when the teacher, in a more adamant tone, demands that the student comply and the student once again refuses or makes a wisecrack. As with all discipline, the two main goals are (1) *get the misbehavior to stop so that you can get back to teaching* and (2) *keep the misbehaving student(s) in class if at all possible*. The following example is a typical beginning for a power struggle:

Teacher: Angel, we need to have a talk. Let's meet after school and discuss how to better handle this situation.
Angel (In front of whole class): I'm not coming; I have a job to do after school.
Teacher (Upset and wanting to show class who is in charge): If I say you will be here, then you will be here. Understand?

Angel (Needing to save face in front of his peers): I won't be here, ever, and you can't make me!

Teacher (Feeling he must win—now the pressure is really on): You will be here or else.

Angel (Aware that the whole class is watching him): Or else what, man? You can't tell me what to do. You're not the boss of me. Go f— yourself!

By the time the teacher and Angel reach this point, they have both risked their pride on the outcome of this power struggle in front of an audience of students. The stakes are high, and although neither wants to lose, it is impossible for either to win. If the teacher forces Angel to come after school, he will make the teacher pay later. If Angel doesn't come, the teacher will feel ridiculed and will punish him later.

Be Aware of How Power Struggles Can Entrap You

Commit yourself to avoiding power struggles. Remember that continuation of a power struggle makes you look foolish and out of control. Be prepared to see long-term victory (a cooperative, positive classroom climate) as more important than short-term winning. By "victory," we mean changing a potentially negative situation into an opportunity for positive communication and mutual trust. It is best to let your students know that you will not stop class each time a student breaks a rule. Sometimes that means letting go of the need for the last word. When establishing rules and consequences, you might say to the entire class, "There will be times when a student breaks a rule, and it may look to you like I am ignoring that student. At those times, know that I will be getting together later with that student to share a proper consequence." Then if a student challenges you in a way that demands a response but you don't want to get trapped, let the class know that you will be dealing later with that student and then redirect attention back to the lesson.

Stay Personally Connected Without Taking It Personally

It is important not to carry anger, resentment, and other hostile feelings once a discipline situation is over. If you are angry with a student from an incident that happened the day before, you might enter a power struggle just to flex your muscles and show who is boss. Instead, try to start fresh each day.

Redirect When Students Are Uncooperative

When a student tries to engage you in a power struggle, set limits, ignore or briefly acknowledge the protest, and then redirect.

Teacher (Walking slowly over to Luther): Luther, in this class we solve problems without making them worse. We do not hit. I will never hit you, and you will never hit anyone. I'll see you later to practice.

Luther: It wasn't my fault, and you can't make me meet with you, ever.

Teacher: That may be. Now, class, who was the only president to resign from office?

In this example, the teacher listened to Luther's protest but did not engage. She gave him a chance to comply by helping him save face. By redirecting, the teacher has opened the door for Luther to comply with the consequence. Before the class was over for the day, the teacher waited by the door and said privately in a calm yet firm voice, "Luther, I look forward to our meeting later."

Acknowledge More Fully the Student's Feelings by Active Listening

In the prior example, the teacher primarily ignored the hook put out by the student. If the student had persisted, or if the teacher preferred to interact more directly to the hooking statement, she might have acknowledged the student's feelings by active listening and reflection.

Teacher (Walking slowly over to Luther): Luther, in this class we solve problems without making them worse. We do not hit. I will never hit you, and you will never hit anyone. I'll see you later to practice.
Luther: It wasn't my fault, and you can't make me meet with you, ever.
Teacher (Slowly beginning to walk back to resume teaching position)
Luther: I said, it wasn't my fault, and you can't make me meet with you, ever. Didn't you hear me?
Teacher (Returning to close proximity to Luther if possible): Luther, you are clearly saying you are not staying, and I can't make you. I can see that you are upset and angry and that you feel that the hitting wasn't your fault. I understand how you might feel. However, this is not the time to discuss it, so let's get back to our lesson, and we can discuss our problem later. Thanks for waiting.

By accepting that the problem was theirs and not only the student's, and by indicating that she understood Luther's feelings, the teacher in this example prevented what might have escalated into a classic power struggle.

Becoming an active listener requires skill and practice. You must be able to step inside the students' experience and develop a sense for the feelings that are motivating their obnoxious behavior. Many troubling situations can be defused by listening with empathy to a student. Active listening means making an educated guess about what a student is feeling and then paraphrasing these feelings by restating them to the student.

Lonny, a student who demonstrated his power by loudly accusing Mr. Gonzales of running a boring class, was sent to the office for such disruptive behavior. Mr. Gonzales feared losing control of the class and felt a need to assert his power. Sending Lonny to the office was his solution, and it was effective in removing the source of the problem, except Lonny was back for more the next day. After Mr. Gonzales had learned how to actively listen, Lonny did his typical routine. But instead of using the standard threat of classroom exclusion, Mr. Gonzales approached Lonny as he continued his lesson and quietly said, "Lonny this class is probably the most boring, awful class you have to attend. It must be a real pain for you to be here. But you are an important member of the class and I'm glad you are here."

After this exchange, Mr. Gonzales immediately returned to the day's lesson, and after the class, the two began a constructive process of discovering what Lonny needed to be less disruptive, and how Mr. Gonzales could be more interesting.

Tell What Is at Stake If the Power Struggle Continues

Often you can defuse a potential power struggle by pointing it out to the student and identifying what is at stake. Neither you nor the student wants to look bad in front of the class, which is what makes it continue.

Teacher: Maria, please put your makeup away and apply it only in the restroom.
Maria (Ignores the teacher and continues to put on her makeup)
Teacher: I can see we have a different opinion of how you should handle your need to look pretty. But I care too much about you to argue and too much about this class to let you continue, so if you can stop for now, I am sure we can find an answer we both like.
Maria: Whatever (as she continues to ignore).
Teacher: If we keep this going, we'll be in an argument that neither of us likes to lose. So thanks for putting the makeup away now. I really appreciate your cooperation.

Get Together Later and Figure Out a Plan to Prevent Future Power Struggles

Meet with the student at a time when there is no audience. Tell the student that you know he sometimes has a problem being corrected. Shake the student's hand while saying, "Wow, we almost got into a real argument in class. Now that we are both calm, I want to let you know that it is never my goal to embarrass you in front of the class. So let's figure out some ways I can get your attention when I need it without embarrassing you."

Students usually want the teacher to be less public and are often willing to accept a nonverbal cue, such as a head nod, so that the misbehaving student will know, but the other students will not. Brainstorm three or four strategies together that help both of you avoid power struggles in the future. When you must implement a consequence with the student, be sure to follow your agreed-on guidelines.

What to Do When More Than One Student Is Acting Out

So far in this chapter we have focused on situations in which the teacher has dealt with a single student who has behaved inappropriately. Sometimes you may be faced with a group of students who are acting out at the same time or feeding off one another. The better you know the dynamics of your class, the more effective you will be in handling this type of situation.

The first step is to pick the one student in the acting-out group who is the one the other students respect the most, fear the most, or are amused by the most. Stopping the misbehavior of this student must come first. We call this strategy "The Leader of the Pack." At a separate time in a one-on-one moment, approach the leader of the pack to help you calm or quiet his crew. Appeal to the student's need for control. Often these students like the role of leader and fit naturally into it. You might say, "Rashid, there is too much talking going on while I am teaching. I need your help solving this problem because I notice that most other students look up to you. What do you think would work?" After suggestions are given, conclude with "I am counting on you to quiet your crew when I give you the signal. Thanks."

If you can get the leader to change, he or she will often bring others along. It is crucial to build a relationship with the leader. Relationship building with the leader needs to be done both in and outside the classroom. Find the student in the hall, a different class, or the lunch room, and have a brief conversation about something other than school. Show up at a play, dance recital, or sporting event that this student is involved in. Doing these things goes a long way in building relationships that will last an entire year.

If you have more than one ringleader, pick the less prominent one first (this gives the most powerful a chance to stop without being dealt with directly), and work at stopping the misbehavior with that student by using one or more of the aforementioned strategies.

Occasionally, you can effectively deal with a whole group. The best time to do this is when they are in close proximity with each other, perhaps working together at a table. Walk over to the group slowly and calmly. Make eye contact with each student before you speak. Then state the rule and consequence scanning the entire group slowly with your eyes. When you are finished, scan the group one more time to make sure they know you are serious and then leave their area. Staying too long while correcting students in a group can often lead to a power struggle.

If you continue to have problems with groups of students, it might be worth your while to have a meeting using the same approach with the leaders as was illustrated with Rashid. You might say, "There is too much talking out of turn going on, and we need to solve this problem. I can continue to nag you and am on the verge of calling home to seek help from your parents, but I am sure there are better ways of fixing this. What are your ideas?" Yelling at the class is rarely effective, because it only leads to more confusion and noise.

When several students in a class are acting out, it is wise to acknowledge a mismatch between the needs of your students and what you are doing or not doing. Sometimes a solution is as simple as walking about the whole room as you present a lesson to keep in close occasional proximity with all students. At other times, you may need to substantially modify your curriculum or method of presentation for change to occur. When you are confronted with a large-group classroom discipline problem, try to maintain an attitude of calm, a security about yourself, and a willingness to explore change.

For the Administrator

Teachers and administrators need to take direct action when rules are broken. Deal with students and teachers the same way you want your teachers to deal with students when they are less than fully cooperative. It can be very difficult for staff not to take offensive behavior from their students personally. You can lead in showing how to stand up to inappropriate behavior without allowing anger and frustration to take over. Set aside time during faculty, department, or team meetings to discuss, teach, and role-play.

During observations, we encourage you to use the list of eight ideas presented in this chapter for taking action as a feedback instrument. As with any observation, it is important to share your plan with the teacher before the observation and receive agreement that this type of feedback will be helpful. Remember that your goal in using the eight ideas is to improve discipline, not to collect information for a formal evaluation.

Help teachers learn how to handle most of their own discipline problems. Sending students to the office not only burdens you and your office staff but also weakens the teacher's leadership. Most infractions can be handled in the classroom if they do not escalate into power struggles. Once they escalate, the teacher usually has no recourse but to kick the student out of the room. Many of the problems sent to you might have been solved by the teacher if not allowed to escalate.

Teachers need to know that the administration will support them if a student fails to accept a consequence. At the same time, set up a policy that gives students a chance to cool off and think before escalation up the ladder begins. You might use a form of this simple model:

1. The teacher gives a consequence.

2. The student refuses, insults the teacher, makes a scene in class, or tries to hook the teacher into a power struggle.

3. The teacher uses a de-escalation strategy, such as
   • Privacy–eye contact–proximity,
   • Redirecting,
   • Active listening,
   • Ignoring or briefly acknowledging the attempt by the student to argue,
   • Speaking with the student later, or
   • Giving the student a time-out (providing a chance for the student to cool down).

4. The teacher gives the student time to think about whether to accept the consequence without pressure or threat.

5. If the student still chooses not to accept the consequence, administration intervenes.

6. The administrator meets with the teacher later to discuss Steps 3 and 4. If the teacher omitted them, provide coaching to help the teacher learn how to include Steps 3 and 4 in the future. If they were included, see if the teacher's skill in using them can be improved. In either case, remember that teachers' main gripes about administration are lack of support with discipline. Coach without reprimanding.

Defusing power struggles is not easy. Emotions run high, and the teacher may not have developed the strength to know how to back away. Teachers need to have their dignity maintained before they can learn to maintain the dignity of their students.

7

Managing Stress Effectively

Teacher stress is higher than at any time we can remember. High-stakes testing, pressure to finish the curriculum, inflexible scripted teaching programs that leave no room for creative innovation, highly structured and labor-intensive behavior programs, along with many other factors, all contribute to stress.

Job-related stress can be handled in two basic ways: change the external causes of it, or change our internal response to it. This chapter focuses on the latter.

Because our state of mind and accompanying behavior are the most important influences on our students, it is important that we manage our feelings of stress so we do not start counting the days until vacation the first day of school! For this reason, we broaden the discussion of stress in this chapter to include some important causes in addition to the challenges posed by disruptive students. In fact, most of the strategies contained in this book, when regularly implemented, have the effect of reducing stress. When students cooperate, we feel good about them and ourselves. Identifying and meeting the basic needs of our students is the single-best way of reducing their stress and ours.

Stress and Discipline

There is no doubt that discipline and stress go hand in hand. According to Antoniou, Polychroni, and Vlachakis (2006), the greatest sources of stress for teachers are problems interacting with students, addressing lack of student interest in school, and handling students with "difficult" behaviors—in essence, problems with motivation and discipline. If we internalize the stress, headaches, exhaustion, sleeplessness, pains, and feelings of inadequacy are among the consequences. If we externalize the stress, we start hating the child and everyone else we deem responsible for aiding or supporting the inappropriate behavior. Teachers overwhelmed by stress often cope by falling into one of the following four categories.

The "Please Like Me" Teacher

Dependent on student approval, these teachers are often willing to ignore misbehavior to continue feeling liked or being seen as cool. They apologetically set limits and rarely follow through with consequences when rules are broken. Such teachers prefer to give themselves headaches, back pains, and other forms of physical tension rather than feel guilty for acting "mean" to their students. Disruptive students see these teachers as weak and ineffective and take control of the classroom because the teachers are at their mercy. This teacher is usually high up on the "wish list" of difficult students because they know life will be easy in this class.

It is good for children to like their teacher. However, when that dynamic becomes the focus, usually the wrong kind of relationship is built. Children respect teachers who are firm, are fair, set limits, and treat them with dignity and respect. Do those things, and students will naturally like you.

The Muscle Flexer

Muscle Flexers adopt the attitude "I do not care if they like me or not, but they'd better do as I want—or else." They often resort to power-based methods, including open confrontation, that invite resistance, retaliation, and rebellion. These teachers are quick to write referrals and inevitably feel that the administration is too soft. Unless these teachers have a warm and caring support system outside school, they are likely to receive so few positive strokes on the job that loss of enthusiasm and early burnout result.

Muscle Flexers like to shout from across the room. They often make examples of students with the hope that others will get the message. Children *hate* this type of teacher, and most Muscle Flexers say they do not care. Muscle Flexers do not have a ton of behavior problems because they usually are successful at getting difficult children removed from their class. They will tell you that their way is effective. We disagree.

The Marine Sergeant

The Marine Sergeant is usually a first cousin to the Muscle Flexer. The prevailing attitude is "Everybody gets treated the same way in here, and there are no exceptions to the rule." Of course, this approach is often taken under the mask of "fairness." Because of the rigidity inherent in this approach, pride often gets in the teacher's way of dealing with tough-to-reach students who read rigidity as an invitation to act out. Although their toughness can be an asset, Marine Sergeants find that they are almost never successful with difficult students because their approach offers no flexibility. This teacher will often knowingly do ineffective things because of a policy or procedure. They are not able to adjust to individual student needs.

The Guilt Giver

There are many ways to feel bad about something wrong you have done. The most productive feeling is remorse. Remorse leads to a commitment to changing behavior. Guilt, in contrast, rarely leads to behavior change. It leads to self-pity, defensiveness, anger, or frustration. The attitude of the Guilt Giver is "Can't you see how miserable I feel when you misbehave? *Pleeeaaase* stop" or "Look at all I'm doing for you, and look at how ungrateful you are!" These teachers lack self-confidence and resort to whining and complaining with hopes that students will come to their senses. Such teachers are personally hurt and angry when students misbehave, but they are unable to express this anger. Limits are set through an appeal to guilt, which is thoroughly ineffective with those students who do not care about your feelings. These teachers are often seen with clenched jaws and fists accompanied by a soft, submissive tone of voice. The students hear the message that they have the power to make the teacher angry, and the worst consequence will be complaining and whining.

Guilt Givers are likely to have numerous interpersonal difficulties because of blocked feelings, which lead to high levels of stress and burnout. This is the most outwardly stressed teacher, often complaining of quitting and telling the world how terrible his job is.

The Discipline-Stress Cycle

We contend that these four teacher types represent the most likely candidates for early burnout. They get out of the profession early to end their unhappiness, or they stay too long and become cynical, apathetic, or angry. They respond to misbehavior ineffectively, which leads to continuation or regression of the problem behavior.

Figure 7.1 illustrates the discipline-stress cycle. It begins when a student acts in a way that interferes with the teaching-learning process. The teacher ineffectively responds by *denying* (pretending not to see or hear misbehavior), *rationalizing* ("I can't expect her to behave herself because of her home situation/history of school failure"), *blaming* ("I saw you do it—it's your fault"), or *provoking* ("I will test your limits as much or more than you test mine"). Each teacher type resorts to one or more of these ineffective methods. When the teacher's corrective response meets with a continuation or worsening of behavior, tension and frustration occur. When these feelings are allowed to accumulate and no relief is in sight, the teacher responds either through withdrawal ("I do not want anything to do with you") or explosive outbursts ("You say that again, and you're out of here!"). Fortunately, there are better alternatives.

Figure 7.1
Discipline and Burnout Cycle

1. Student Behavior
2. Ineffective teacher response
   a. blaming
   b. rationalizing
   c. provoking
   d. denying
   e. taking revenge (I must be in control, I'll get even)
3. No student improvement, or worsening
4. Teacher tension and frustration
5. Withdrawal or explosive behavior by the teacher
6. Increased misbehavior by the students
7. Burnout

Strategies for Reducing Stress Caused by Students

Anticipate the Predictable

A major key in effectively handling our stress is to stop being surprised at what students say and do! Teaching can be unpredictable in that unexpected things happen every day. Yet, it is interesting that in many ways teaching is highly predictable. You know the exact days of the week you are going to work, the exact hours you will be there, and the exact location you are going to be in. You know your "customers" will come every single day, whether you are good or not. You can even closely estimate how much money you are going to make the first day of your first year on the job! Despite such predictability, amazingly, we still are surprised by what children do and say.

For example, what happens nearly each time a teacher corrects a student and then attempts to walk away? What does every child in the world do under his breath? Predictably and with attitude, he mumbles something barely loud enough to hear, but not usually loud enough to make a scene. Unfortunately, many teachers hear the mumbling and get trapped by their stress. Trying to protect their authority they stop, turn around and provocatively ask, "What did you say to me, young man?" And what does every child say back? One of two things: Your not-so-difficult students say, "Nothing." Your really tough children say, "I called you an as*h**e." Either way, tension increases. One way to reduce stress is by understanding how much we contribute to it through failure to anticipate the predictable. Because nothing good ever comes from asking a student, "What did you say?" stop confronting with this question! Make it your policy that if you think you heard it, you heard it, and be prepared to respond to what you heard.

Anticipating what students will say and do in predictable situations can greatly reduce, if not eliminate, the stress we allow children to cause us. Embarrassing them in front of their friends, yelling at them from across the room, forcing them to do work that is too hard, and requiring ridiculously strict rules to be followed (especially if they make no sense) will guarantee nasty remarks from certain students. A power struggle is likely, which naturally creates more stress, tension, and misery.

We recently consulted in an elementary school outside Hilton Head, South Carolina. Before asking us to work with four teachers who were struggling with discipline, the principal wanted us to watch the teacher she considered to be the best in the school. Ms. Evans was about 5′5″ and 100 pounds. Her white teeth gleamed as she greeted us with the same cheerful "Good morning" that met each of her students. About midway through her math lesson, a young boy in the back threw a wadded-up piece of paper at a girl two desks away. Ms. Evans turned around just in time to see the release of the paper and the girl get hit. The entire class watched to see what she would do. Ms. Evans immediately instructed the students to "put their eyes back on their own papers." She then walked over to Taniq, the boy who threw the paper. As privately as possible, in a firm yet nonaggressive tone she said, "Throwing things at other people in this class is unacceptable. What can we do to make sure this does not happen again?" Taniq looked back at Ms. Evans and said, "I hate this stupid class. It is so boring, and besides, I have no idea what I'm doing, anyway." Ms. Evans replied, "After class we will talk about this privately, and I promise I will make things better for you in here. But for now, what do you think you should say to Yolanda [the girl hit by the paper]?"

After class we met with Ms. Evans to explore how she was able to handle this incident so well. She defused the student, kept him in class, got everyone else back on track, and even got Taniq to apologize without telling him to do so. Our conversation went like this:

Consultants: Weren't you offended when he threw the paper, said he hated your class, and called it boring?

Ms. Evans: No. He's 8. That's what some 8-year-olds do.

Consultants: I know. But what he said and did was inappropriate. Didn't it make you the least bit upset?

Ms. Evans: No. He's 8. That's what some 8-year-olds do.

Consultants (a bit disbelieving): So you didn't get the least bit upset?

Ms. Evans (smiling): Not the least bit. He's 8. That's what some 8-year-olds do. And besides, no 8-year-old can make me mad unless I let them. And I'm not giving Taniq that kind of power.

By knowing what "some 8-year-olds do" before they do it, Ms. Evans was able to handle this situation in a respectful and dignified way. She did not get upset or angry and was not the least bit stressed-out by this event. Ms. Evans summed up the key to not getting stressed by stating simply, "He's 8. That's what some 8-year-olds do. No 8-year-old can get me mad unless I let them." Some children swear, others are rude, a few are forgetful, some won't be able to sit still for very long, and others will struggle to understand the material. Having an idea of what they are going to do before they do it helped Ms. Evans and can help you when working with this type of class.

We believe the images that create stress are a mind-set. It is in the head. It is part of the imagination. It is not real unless we let it become real. Some children are good at causing stress, but only because they know exactly what to do and say to push our buttons. But since predictability works both ways, we have to be a step ahead of our students. We can know what they are going to do to try and stress us out and then be sure not to show the least bit of stress, anger, or anguish. Instead, we can smile and say, "I'm smiling because I knew you were going to say that. If you want to get the reaction you're looking for, get to class on time, bring your books, and be polite. I promise then I'll be shocked!"

Do Not Take Inappropriate Behavior Personally

We believe the best strategy for stress management is controlling your attitude! If you perfect this one strategy, you can skip to the next chapter because stress caused by students will dramatically decrease. *Stay personally connected to children, without taking personally what children do and say.*

Let's dissect this advice: *Stay personally connected to children.* You might even hang up the following pledge or at least keep it handy as a self-reminder:

> I will not give up on you.
>
> I will not quit on you.
>
> I will not lose control with you.
>
> I will not yell at you.
>
> I will not be angry at you.
>
> I will always be here no matter what.
>
> Because I am a teacher and my job is to show you a better way,
>
> I will not take personally what you do or say when I do not like it.

The best teachers are smart enough to know that objectionable behavior is not about them. Somewhere some students learned to talk that way. They learned to hit instead of use words. They were taught that the way they are behaving is actually the right way. We all have our buttons. When you feel yours are getting pushed, before reacting try hearing or seeing what the student said or did in a more neutral way or even silly way. For example, imagine the student called you a "chair" rather than an "a*sh*le." Our immediate reaction would be to feel concern for the student rather than anger at her disrespect.

Develop Mental Toughness

People who are the best at their jobs, whatever the profession, stay calm in the face of pressure. They focus on what they need to do, not on circumstances out of their control. Teachers can decide that students are not going to get to them. They can measure success on a weekly, daily, or hourly basis. When students get more stressed, the teacher can choose to get calmer. Great teachers expect certain behaviors based on the type of class they have, the time of day, the subject, the parent involvement, and the hundreds of other factors involved when you have 25 different minds, 25 different feelings, and 25 different home lives.

Stress Busters During the Day

The next two chapters will describe several more teaching strategies. But the ones presented here will help directly reduce stress. These strategies are basic, they do not take much prep time, and they are easy to implement.

Network with a Colleague

Sending children to the principal will almost always increase stress over the long haul. Remember, as soon as you send a child to the office, the outcome is out of your hands. It is not OK to get annoyed or mad at administrators for what they decide to do, even if you disagree. If you do not like how they handle discipline problems, then stop sending your children to them.

When you need a break, consider networking with a trusted colleague. A fellow teacher, school counselor, psychologist, or social worker can be a huge help. Develop prearranged signals with this person that will tell them what kind of support you are looking for. For example, if a student ever comes down with the yellow pass, it means "I need a break from the child for 10 minutes." If a student comes down with a purple scarf, it means "I'm ready to totally lose it and need about 20 minutes." Most of the time when children come back to the classroom, they are at least a little bit calmer than when they left. You will sometimes even get an off-the-cuff "sorry" from the student as she re-enters your room. If possible, it is best to set this system up with someone who is not a regular teacher so that you know this person is available during class time. Teachers who do this tell us that just knowing they have a place to send a student gives them peace of mind and that they almost never end up having to use it.

Become Predictably Unpredictable

Wear silly clothes; teach from the back of the room; give the children a "free homework makeup day"; go on field trips; sing songs; play games (that are not competitive); dance; rap. Most important, enjoy yourself and have fun. The best teachers are able to change things up. They do different activities, bring in guest speakers, and use real-life shows and events to teach what might otherwise be viewed as boring monotony.

For example, one of the authors can remember only one lesson from 16 years ago in 9th grade earth science. In fact, it is pretty much the only lesson remembered from high school (sorry to all my former teachers). Our teacher took us on a field trip to the minor league baseball stadium. Upon arrival we met the head groundskeeper. He taught us why the grass in the stadium was so perfectly maintained and how to get certain colors and looks. He showed us the difference between the soil used on the infield and the dirt most high school fields used. He explained the drainage system and why it can rain for an entire day and within two hours the outfield is completely bone-dry. You've never seen a group of 9th graders so interested in grass and dirt. When we got back to school, our teacher asked us to pull out the textbooks so he could reinforce what we just learned. While not every unit began with a trip to the ball park, this teacher was notorious for showing us first and telling us later. And besides, it is not possible to be stressed when your day includes a field trip to the baseball stadium!

Create an "I'm Good At" Board

This strategy was created by a stressed-out teacher who was sick and tired of her students constantly asking her for help. So at the beginning of the year, she created an "I'm good at" board. The teacher had each student write at least one thing he or she was good at in school and one thing the student was good at outside school.

The teacher then posted each student's name on a large board. Under each name she listed the two things that the person was good at. Before any student was allowed to ask her for help in the classroom, the student had to consult the "I'm good at" board. If a fellow classmate was good at the thing the questioning student was struggling with, he was required to ask that classmate for help first. If that person was not able to help or was busy working on something else, the student could then ask the teacher. This was a great way to get students to know each other. It also gave the children a place to go with their questions without constantly nagging the teacher. Nagging children often lead to stress and burnout!

The board is also great for new students who come in midway through the year. They can check the board and see with which students they might naturally have things in common. You might learn that the new student likes basketball and introduce him to two others who like it as well.

Write a "Dear Clarence" Letter

Clarence, a teacher of emotionally disturbed students in West Palm Beach, thought of this one. Students write down a question or a problem they are having in the class. They begin the question or problem by writing "Dear Clarence." Once a week Clarence pulls a problem or question from the box and addresses it with the class. The students are encouraged to work together to figure out an answer to the problem or question. Clarence told us that by having an outlet for their questions, student complaining dramatically decreased.

WHEN STUDENTS COMPLAIN ABOUT OTHER TEACHERS

Sometimes you will be a sounding board for children complaining about other teachers. This is fine as long as you are always helping students see how the problem is theirs. For example, a student comes to you and says, "I hate Mr. Z. He's such a jerk. I can't believe he makes us do all this work. He's so unfair, too. Seriously, can you believe that? I think the work he gives us is stupid!" No matter how you feel about that teacher, the only proper response is something like this:

> I'm sorry you think he's unfair. And you are right. You do not have to do the work in his class. But let's just agree right now that not doing the work means you will fail. That is a guarantee. And if you fail, you'll get to go through this all over again next year. Is that what you want?
>
> In life you will have to work for people you like, and people you do not. Part of growing up is succeeding in both places. If you want, I'm OK with having you complain and let off steam here, but I would rather teach you some strategies you can use to be successful in his class. Are you interested?

Do not talk negatively about teachers to your students. It makes you look bad and is of no help to anyone. Instead, help the student work through the problem, even if you totally agree with her assessment of the teacher.

Other Teachers and Stress

In trainings, teachers often ask us how they can change other teachers who disagree with them. It is important to understand that as a teacher, it is not our job to change other teachers. For the most part, we recommend minding your own business. We can share ideas, collaborate, agree, or disagree. We can even attempt to influence change in colleagues by explaining or showing how their life might actually improve if they do things differently. What *we can insist* on, however, is the banning of toxic talk and actions that can create an extremely negative atmosphere when allowed to occur. We all have a right to perform in a toxic-free environment. Just as individuals have a right to smoke in their own homes but not in a smoke-free public restaurant, if teachers want to complain about or call students names, it should be banned in "public" places like the faculty room and at a staff meeting. We know of one school's faculty room that got so toxic with anti-everybody sentiment, most of the noncomplaining teachers preferred to eat alone in their classrooms. Bucking the trend, one of the brave young teachers was first to the faculty room during his lunch hour and sat alone at first at a table with a sign that read, "No Talking About Students Allowed at This Table." Within minutes, that table was half-filled; within a few days, another had to be added.

We recommend that all teachers fight cynicism in their school. What would happen if you said to a teacher, "That sounded cynical. Can you say it in another way so you won't be misunderstood?"

Administrators and Stress

Here are a few things you can do so that administrators do not stress you out:

• **Invite them in.** Make it very clear that they are always welcome to stop in your room. Most administrators will not take you up on it. If they do, that's fine, too. But either way, you look good.

• **Include them as a participant in class activities during an observation.** Many teachers will ask an administrator if they "want to be part of an activity." Say instead, "In this room everyone participates in what we are doing. Which group would like to have, Ms. Principal?" If the administrator protests, do not back down. Remember, inside that classroom you are the boss. It is your name on the door. Make them a part of what is going on in your room. If parents are present, then they participate as well. We promise, if nothing else, including others will gain you a ton of respect from your students and usually from your administrator.

• **Explain how your room works.** Let them know the policies and procedures that you have ahead of time. For example, tell your principal, "In my room I do my best to be fair to each of my students, which means I do not treat them all exactly the same way. I also will not discuss one child with someone else's parent." By doing this, you show strong leadership and organizational skills.

• **Tell them you will do your best to handle your own problems and keep children in class.** We've never met an administrator who disagrees with this tip, although some may have a different view of what constitutes an appropriate referral. Share your social contract and explain circumstances that may require you to ask for administrative support.

• **Complaining is ineffective!** Instead of complaining, present a plan for how to fix the situation. Many teachers are good at telling everyone what is wrong but offer few solutions to problems. Good administrators will give you what you are asking for if you present a well-thought-out idea with a solution. For example, some teachers will say, "I already have 28 students, and the contract says that is the max. Sorry—I'm not taking him." That statement will probably get the child to go elsewhere, but it will also get an administrator annoyed with you. Instead, try saying the following: "I already have 28 students in my class, and I'd be glad to take the 29th. However, I think it would cause a huge disturbance in our class because I just now have them working well together. Adding a new body at this time is likely to be a huge disruption. I've already spoken with Ms. Hall, and she is willing to take him. However, we will work closely to monitor his progress, and he will even come to my room sometimes for XYZ." In the second approach, you are not complaining and instead are proposing a solution. You thus have a much better chance of being heard.

For the Administrator

Stress, like discipline, is an intrinsic part of the teacher's everyday school experience; and, also like discipline, many teachers are reluctant to admit their feelings of stress because they do not want to be considered weak or ineffective. Keep an open dialogue with your staff, making it very clear that they can talk to you about anything related to their job, even if their problem is with you, their boss.

Have fun and laugh with your teachers. According to Hurren (2006), principals who share humor in the workplace have teachers with higher job satisfaction than those principals who share very little or no humor in the workplace.

As an administrator, your main concern related to teacher stress is to help identify the causes and provide strategies for dealing with them. One school reduced stress by tackling the problem of student movement within its relatively open campus. The solutions cut down on students interrupting classes by yelling and running through the halls during instructional time, which staff had determined was a major stressor.

If you identify teachers who are highly stressed, take the time to offer guidance and comfort. Support them and look for ways you can help. Let them know that you agree there is a lot to cover and not a ton of time. Help teachers decipher between what is critical and what they might be able to leave out.

Offer to teach or take over a difficult class once in a while, and after the experience, acknowledge the motivational and disciplinary difficulties posed by some students before offering either advice or suggestions.

Teachers, like administrators, often feel ignored and unappreciated. Generous and sincere compliments can trigger weeks of enthusiasm. We recently met a principal who surprised his staff by bringing in a "chair masseuse." They were given the afternoon of an in-service day off and were encouraged to get a free 15-minute head, neck, and shoulder massage in the school lobby.

At a recent seminar in Dallas, the principal left a little early to begin grilling lunch. Everyone had steak, chicken, and hamburgers cooked to order by the principal.

Another way to deal with stress is through physical activity. Provide outlets by opening the gymnasium and other facilities for faculty use. Help organize both formal and informal exercise groups, dance groups, basketball and volleyball games, jogging, Frisbee, and other fun activities. When setting physical stress reduction activities, you might want to include your physical education staff to help develop a program similar to the one described here. In many instances, all it takes to spur a sense of renewal among teachers is to be positively noticed and sincerely appreciated by their building administrator.

8

Strategies for Students Who Chronically Misbehave

In response to the question "What do you want to do when you graduate high school?" several 7th graders from a gang- and drug-infested neighborhood answered, "Go to prison." When asked why, they responded, "It's cool. You earn your bones" (a prison expression meaning you get respect).

It is now common to have special needs students blended into regular classes so that virtually all teachers have students who 10 or 20 years ago would not have been mainstreamed. Most schools now require all teachers to provide differentiated instruction to this diverse population of students. More regular education children come to school with baggage that can dramatically affect the school climate.

Earlier editions of this book referred to this chapter as "Creative Discipline for Out-of-Control Students" to emphasize the need to get beyond the "same old, same old" with children who continually do not respond to more traditional methods. The focus was on particularly difficult students. Although this focus still holds, we prefer referring to these creative interventions as "unconventional" because all students can benefit from a creative teacher, but not all students need unconventional approaches to elicit better choices. For example, all students can benefit from exercise, but only a limited few need exercise to become better focused. To increase our influence, educators must have both conventional and unconventional strategies. This chapter provides both.

It seems that every year most teachers have at least a few students who appear to thrive on setting up one power struggle after another as they disrupt the learning process. They are the students who loudly complain of the teacher's unfairness, who make various noises, who show up to class unprepared, who are quick to lose their temper, and who simply refuse to take responsibility for their actions. The teacher finds himself at wit's end with these students and often proclaims, "Somebody's got to do something with that child!" Many of these students believe themselves to be inferior, inadequate, and unworthy, yet they hide these feelings from themselves and others through destructive behaviors that make them feel in control.

These students typically function well below grade level despite having adequate intellectual potential. Others are chronically angry (many with good reason) and respond with anger to real or imagined insult and attacks.

Although factors outside school are often at the foundation of such problems, these students generally find the school environment unresponsive to their needs. Because their lives are rooted in confusion and powerlessness, they resent a system that tells them what to do, how to do it, and how well they have done.

Other chapters have described a comprehensive process for discipline prevention and effective actions to be taken when students break rules or refuse to accept consequences. When methods of prevention are insufficient, it is necessary to interrupt the inappropriate behavior. Although there are no perfect ways to effectively manage the chronically misbehaving student, a plethora of interventions can help. Many of the interventions we share will help build confidence and add excitement to the often-draining process of attempting to manage the behavior of students who seem motivated to mostly drive you crazy.

These interventions include negotiation strategies in which student and teacher (sometimes one or more resource personnel, teachers, or parents are included) find ways to make life more acceptable for everyone. Other interventions with more of an instructional focus aim to teach students better social, problem-solving, impulse control, and self-regulation skills. Some are paradoxically designed to "confuse" a student into exploring healthier behavior. A few include traditional behavior modification techniques that can help teach more appropriate behaviors despite the many caveats we have discussed throughout this book in using such methods. Helping children acquire skills needed for success in life always trumps philosophy.

Negotiation Strategies

Students who continually misbehave often need individualized help to learn how to follow the classroom rules. Some of these students respond well with efforts to elicit their cooperation through negotiation. Positive student confrontation and the family intervention process are two such negotiation methods.

Positive Student Confrontation

Positive student confrontation is a mediation process that involves setting aside time to meet individually with a student in an attempt to resolve differences by negotiating. It is a time-consuming process; thus, it is best done with students who take excessive class time because of their misbehavior. To be effective, teachers must be willing to view student misbehavior as a symptom of conflict between teacher and student, listen to a student's complaints, and show some degree of flexibility. The idea is to find solutions that are good for both sides.

Although a meeting or series of meetings between the teacher and student can be sufficient, it is usually best to involve a *neutral* third person who can guide both parties to find common ground that can make things better for each. This person may be another teacher, counselor, administrator, resource person, or even another student. The important attributes of the third person are being a good listener and being able to remain calm when the going gets rough. We refer to this mediator as a "coach."

The process includes the teacher and student taking turns telling each other dislikes, likes, and wants. After each step, the listener is asked to repeat the statement to ensure understanding. Once all of the information is presented, solutions are sought. When a plan of action is determined, each person is requested to sign an individual contract, and another meeting is scheduled to check how well the plan is working.

Individual negotiation requires the aggrieved teacher to be willing to

- Share directly with the student,
- Risk hearing unpleasant things from the student, and
- Consider program modifications for the student.

It also comes with the fundamental belief that student opinions, ideas, and thoughts are important and will be valued, listened to, and even acted on in this classroom. Before positive student confrontation begins, it can be extremely helpful for the coach to discuss the process with each party separately so each knows what to expect. The specific guidelines for positive student confrontation are as follows:

1. The coach (third party) describes the problem, process, and his or her role. For example: "I understand there are some things going on in the classroom that are making it hard for you, Mrs. Jones, to teach, and hard for you, Joe, to follow the rules. I'm here to see if we can find a way to feel better about being together in here."

2. The coach encourages both the teacher and student to share feelings of dislike, resentment, anger, or frustration. For example, the coach says to the teacher, "This may not be easy, but tell Joe what he says or does that makes it hard for you to teach." After responding, the coach then addresses the student.

For example: "Tell Mrs. Jones what goes on in the classroom that makes it hard for you to follow the rules." After each side has a turn, each is encouraged to repeat or paraphrase the other's statements so that an understanding of concerns is ensured. (Paraphrasing applies to subsequent steps as well.)

3. The teacher and student share appreciations. ("Tell what you like or appreciate about Mrs. Jones.")

4. The teacher and student make demands. ("Tell what you want Joe to do differently from what he is doing right now.")

5. The teacher and student negotiate a solution. ("Tell what you are willing to do differently that you think can help solve this problem.")

6. Agreement is reached, put in writing, and signed.

7. Evaluation responsibilities are established so that each side can keep track of how well the agreement is working.

8. A meeting for follow-up is scheduled.

The coach needs to be aware that both sides usually come with a list of complaints that feed their frustrations. It is important in these cases that the coach asks them to list only the two or three things that they most want to see changed. This keeps the process manageable for all involved. If by the end of a session both sides can agree to make small but clear changes, that success can be used as a building block to pave the way toward resolving other concerns.

Family Intervention Process

The family intervention process is a collaborative effort among school personnel, parents, and the student to define concrete and reachable goals, and positive or negative consequences contingent on goal attainment. Goals must be specific, measurable, and reachable. The steps are as follows.

1. Meet with parent(s). If the child lives in a two-parent home, strongly request a meeting with both. If the student is living with a single parent, then meet alone or include any and all extended family or live-in adults who provide frequent child-rearing activities. In most cases, the student should be present as well. All people at the meeting are invited to be active problem-solving participants. At this meeting, be sure to stress that you want to help the child be more successful. Do not blame the child or parent. Say things like "I want the student to

"Stay awake in class";

"Be on time";

"Participate in class activities."

2. Be certain that the problem is lack of effort. For example, make sure you know the student has the ability to perform the behavior but is choosing not to. Decide which problem to tackle first. Because this is a powerful intervention, asking the child to reach an unattainable goal will only make things much worse.

3. Set a concrete goal that is measurable and can be reached in a short amount of time. For example, the student will be in class on time and complete at least 80 percent of the next two homework assignments.

4. Establish positive and negative consequences for reaching or failing to reach the goal. The student and parents are important partners in identifying what these are and where they will be implemented.

5. Consider making the plan into a written contract in which the student says what she agrees to do, what she will receive if successful, and what she will lose if unsuccessful.

6. Decide on how you will monitor the student's progress and what kinds of follow-up will be done (e.g., sending home daily or weekly reports; setting a date for the next meeting).

Reinforcement of Key Social Skills

Key social skills are frequently lacking in students who get into trouble. Persistence is necessary because chronically misbehaving students are often locked into behaviors that have become automatic but inappropriate in a school setting. It is beyond the scope of this book to offer a curriculum on social skills training. Many solid programs are available (e.g., Goldstein, 1999; Henley, 2003). Instead, we offer tips on basic social skills that we know are especially necessary and are frequently lacking among students who get into trouble.

Most of these strategies can be taught informally by virtually all teachers without requiring a curriculum. Many of the skills described here can also be shared as components of your classroom procedures. Just as athletic coaches and directors of school plays know the value of practice repetitions for the skill to be mastered under real conditions, the same is true for social skills, especially if these skills are not a regular part of home life. Students respond best in a trusting atmosphere because they are learning and practicing skills that often take time to master.

Key Social Skills

• **Greeting others.** Children in trouble rarely say, "Good morning," "Nice to see you," "Hi," or "Have a nice day." Instead of complaining about their bad manners, we advocate teaching them these skills.

• **Showing eye contact.** Children with poor social skills need practice making eye contact. Even students for whom eye contact is a cultural negative (including many Asians and Native Americans) can benefit from learning that eye contact with certain people can help get them what they need in the larger culture. Naturally, we can be sensitive to the cultural component while simultaneously exploring where, when, and with whom this skill can be of benefit.

• **Making a request.** Teach children to start a request with "Please" or "I would appreciate." Also remind them to close a request with "Thank you."

• **Getting someone's attention.** This skill is best achieved with words like "Excuse me," or "I'd like to tell you what I think."

• **Following instructions.** Share with your students that before they do something, they need first to listen to directions. Then they need to repeat back each step of the directions before doing the task.

• **Accepting criticism.** This social skill is about students learning they do not have to argue or deny when somebody says something critical. They can simply say, "Thanks for the feedback," and either accept or dismiss it.

• **Resisting peer pressure.** Here are a few easy lines students can learn to use when they do not want to join in but are feeling pressured:

"Thanks for the offer and I'd really like to, but unfortunately I can't."

"Not now. I have really bad luck, and probably I'd get caught and mess it up for everybody."

"Unfortunately I can't right now, but maybe some other time."

Self-Control Strategies

Most successful students learn to quietly verbalize what they think, and they use these verbalizations to guide their academic and social behaviors. In their own minds, they are able to say such things as "I need to raise my hand" so they do not blurt out, and "I'm mad right now, but if I hit her, I'll get into trouble, and that isn't worth it." By contrast, students in frequent trouble need specific help in learning how to use language before they behave. Furthermore, it is virtually always necessary to pair verbalizing with mental rehearsal and role playing so students can anticipate problem situations and then practice what to say or do (Henley, 2003). Self-verbalizing typically involves teaching the student to ask questions of himself about the nature of the problem, give himself instructions about performance of the task, and provide appropriate reinforcement and corrective feedback. Lots of practice is often necessary for this skill to become internalized. Let's take a look at some of the original programs, because virtually all later approaches incorporate some or all of their elements (Mendler, 2005).

Think Aloud

When encountering a problem, children are trained to ask themselves the following questions and provide an answer before asking the next question (Camp, Blom, Herbert, & Van Doorninck, 1977):

1. What is my problem?
2. What is my plan to solve the problem?
3. Am I using my plan?
4. How did I do?

Problem Solving

This approach, first developed by Meichenbaum (1977), includes the following questions and statements:

1. What am I supposed to do?
2. I need to look at all possibilities.
3. I have to focus and concentrate.
4. I have to make a choice.
5. How well did I do?

Adolescent Anger Control

In adolescent anger control (Feindler & Ecton, 1986), the student takes these steps:

1. Identify direct (provocations by another person) and indirect (thinking someone is being unfair or lying) anger triggers.

2. Identify physiological states related to anger (e.g., getting hot, sweating, clenching hands, tightening facial muscles, etc.).

3. Practice relaxation methods (e.g., counting backward, taking deep breaths, taking a walk, etc.).

4. Use cognitive-behavioral methods (e.g., reminders such as "Chill out," "Take it easy," "Just stay calm," or "It's not worth the hassle").

5. Conduct an evaluation, asking yourself, "How did I do?" (e.g., "I did well"; "I kept in control"; "I did OK"; "I felt like killing him, and I only said _____ —I can do even better next time"; "I lost it. Next time this happens, I'll need to remind myself to _____.").

Reminders Through Acronyms

Many people remember the names of the Great Lakes through the acronym HOMES (Huron, Ontario, Michigan, Erie, Superior). Students can use acronyms as well to more easily and quickly remember the steps involved in maintaining self-control when problems occur. Some examples follow:

STOMA:

> **S**top before you do anything.
>
> **T**ake a breath; then think about what happened and what you want to do.
>
> **O**ptions: what are the consequences of each choice?
>
> **M**ove on it (make a choice).
>
> **A**ppreciate yourself (for not losing control and doing your best).

WIN:

> **W**hat is the problem?
>
> **I**dentify possible solutions.
>
> **N**arrow it down to the best choice.

TAG:

> **T**ell someone what they are doing to bother you.
>
> **A**sk them to stop.
>
> **G**o tell someone if they do not.

QTIP: Quit **T**aking **I**t **P**ersonally

STAR: Stop; **T**hink; **A**ct; **R**eview

Two Powerful Questions

You can also teach self-control by asking your students:

1. What do people say or do that makes you feel mad?
2. Why do you think people say or do these things?

The first question elicits many spontaneous responses from students, such as "When others do not share," "Name-calling," "Taking my stuff," and "Calling my mama names." It is usually best for the teacher to list these responses and then guide discussion to the second question, varying your next question depending on the age of the student:

With older students: "When others say or do these things, are they trying to *give you power*, or are they trying to *rob you of your power*?"

With younger students: "Are they trying to make you feel weak or strong?"

With very young children: "Are they trying to make you feel happy or sad?"

Follow this with brainstorming, presenting, and/or teaching strategies that can help students find ways of handling these types of difficult situations without getting into trouble. You might introduce assertion strategies from the next section as examples.

Assertion Techniques

Teaching students to substitute *assertive* behavior for *aggressive* behavior can be a turning point in gaining feelings of control and power. Strategies need to be taught and practiced so students can master these techniques.

Walking Away Assertively

We especially recommend practicing this technique because it is much easier said than done. Express understanding of how the desire for respect and need for pride can get in the way of walking away. Connect walking away as a skill to keep your own power so that you do not give power away to someone who wants to make you feel badly. Teachers then need to model this approach when they are in a situation that requires walking away.

Here is a strategy to make walking away more palatable.

REDEFINING THE ATTACKER

If a student hits because he was called a name (e.g., Lee calls Erin a baby), try a dialogue like the following:

Teacher (privately to Erin): If I call you a pencil, are you a pencil?
Erin: No.
Teacher: What are you?
Erin: A girl.
Teacher: If I call you a book, does that mean you are a book?
Erin: No.
Teacher: What are you?
Erin: A girl.
Teacher: If someone calls you a baby, are you a baby?
Erin: No.
Teacher: What are you?
Erin: A girl.
Teacher: Can you walk away from someone who cannot tell the difference between a girl and a baby?

I-Messages

Students can use I-messages to assert themselves with other students and with their teacher. It is usually enough to say, "I do not like it when _____. Please stop."

   Then walk away.

The Bug/Want Strategy

This strategy teaches students to say what bugs them and what they want. For example: "It *bugs* me when you push me. I *want* you to stop."

Escalated Assertion

These gradually intensifying responses can be taught to students:

"Please give me my book back."

"I asked you to give me my book back."

"I know you want that book, but it belongs to me, and I want it back."

"If I don't get my book back, we'll probably both get into trouble, so thanks for giving it back."

"Hassling with you over the book isn't worth it" (walks away and worries about the book later).

Quick Comebacks

Prepare students with easy-to-learn responses they can use when somebody is picking on them or trying to bait them into an argument. We offer a few examples:

"I'm sorry you feel that way."

"I wish you felt different."

"That is your opinion."

"I'm sorry if I did something to make you mad."

"I didn't mean to bother you, and I am sorry if I did."

"You are right, and I apologize."

Behavior Modification: The Daily Student Rating Card

The best use of traditional methods of behavior modification is to form a bridge toward developing better self-control. Students who have not internalized proper behavior and who are continuously disruptive or dangerous to others may need more immediate tangible gratification in the form of points, privileges, or classic rewards while learning how to conduct themselves appropriately. There are significant risks in using any reward program, including teaching manipulative techniques to children and teaching them to rely on others to know what's best and to think you get something for doing right. Therefore, caution is advised.

A daily student rating card (see Figure 8.1) may be used to rate and monitor agreed-upon behavior established through one of the negotiation strategies. It can also be used entirely as its own method. The day is arranged by class period or subject, and the student is rated in relevant categories. Each rating is associated with a certain number of points that can be accumulated. The ratings are tallied, and positive or negative consequences are implemented either at home or at school.

At the beginning of the program or as the student shows improvement, the responsibility for rating and consequence selection is either shared with or given to the student. For example, after a period of relative compliance requiring close teacher monitoring, the next step is to give the student an opportunity to do her own ratings while you do yours. Next, the student does her own ratings independently after a period of relative agreement between the teacher's ratings and her own. Finally, the program is discontinued because the behavior has been internalized and the student "graduates."

Figure 8.1
Daily Rating Chart

Name _____ Date _____

Please rate this child in each of the areas listed below using ratings of 1 to 4.

| 1 = Excellent | 2 = Good | 3 = Fair | 4 = Poor |

Class Periods/Subject

Area	1	2	3	4	5	6	Comments
Classroom Participation							
Cooperation							
Class assignments							
Homework							
Peer interaction							

1 = 5 points   2 = 3 points   3 = 1 point   4 = 0 points

Note: This chart is adapted from Barkley, 1981

Unconventional Strategies

Teachers often relate to challenging students in very predictable ways: we give up, or we are argumentative. The main purpose of an unconventional strategy is to interrupt the flow of disruptive behavior by saying and doing things that force the student to find new ways of fulfilling her needs for connection and control. Because these strategies are purposely designed to confuse the student into developing new patterns of behavior and interaction, they are initially outside our comfort zone and usually require considerable practice before using. We recommend them when more conventional methods just don't work.

Legitimize the Problem Behavior

Teacher opposition to problem behavior is the fuel that feeds most students who chronically misbehave. The more we object, criticize, blame, and punish, the stronger the very behavior that we want to stop becomes. Implementing ways to unemotionally redirect the behavior can have much more success. When behavior occurs excessively, we have a better chance of ending it when it is allowed but redirected. There can be wisdom in permitting five minutes of "social time" to a class that is endlessly chatting or an opportunity for the class clown to tell his three best jokes every day.

Use Coupons to Legitimize

Except for aggressive behaviors that can be harmful to others, coupons can be used to manage excessive behaviors you find objectionable. Give a targeted student a limited number of coupons to perform the very behavior she already excessively does. For example, a student who constantly complains may be given five complaint coupons (initially the number of coupons should be close to but less than what is done on average). At a relatively private moment, the teacher says something like this:

> Jenny, you have a lot of ideas about how to make the class better. At the same time, it's hard for me to listen as much as I would like several times a day. So I'm giving you four suggestion coupons to use. Just give me a coupon each time you're going to say something you don't like about the class or have a suggestion about how to make it better.

This approach can be used for many types of behaviors—talking out of turn, making excuses, tapping a pencil, not doing homework, getting out of seat, and so forth.

Reverse Roles

Many teachers have used the technique of allowing a student to play teacher for a short time. This strategy is designed to carry that concept one step further. If a student is making it difficult for you to teach, give him the responsibility of teaching your class for a significant time period. For example:

> "Lou, I can't teach when you shout, and I am sure you can do a better job than me. Here is the chalk."

Most students will seem hesitant to be in charge and will back off, usually stopping their inappropriate behavior. When they do, simply resume teaching. If they take over, sit in a different seat but otherwise act at least as badly as the student usually does. Most students stop after a very brief period. Some will actually continue and do a decent job teaching.

After the experience, meet privately with the student to try to solve your conflicts. Some students are amazed to see a mirror image (or worse) of how they usually behave. This approach can open the door to developing a plan or contract for improved decision making.

Use Humor and Nonsense

Write down various jokes, phrases, sayings, and statements that you find funny or nonsensical. Try to include in your list some that are certain to get a rise from many of your students. Perhaps familiarize yourself with the rhythm of rap so you can create a line related to a student. At least once per day for one week when a student behaves disruptively, respond with one of your funny statements. For example, as Jack comes to class late for the third day in a row, tell him poetically, "Jack! Jack! Good to see you back. I was beginning to wonder when you would thunder." A student in Sue Freeman's class in Philadelphia recently asked why he had to "learn this dumb junk." Her answer was "(1) The school district and state say I have to teach it. (2) Here is their phone number—when you know why we have to do it, please tell us all!"

Humor is a characteristic often noted among teachers who have excellent rapport with their students (Loomans & Kolberg, 2002; Lundberg & Thurston, 2002). More than 30 years ago, Moscowitz and Hayman (1974) found that those teachers rated "best" by inner-city high school students used more humor than did those rated "typical." Other characteristics of "best" teachers were those who

- Discussed current events in class,
- Did not yell while disciplining, and
- Were able to empathize with student feelings.

Agree with the Put-down, Criticism, or Accusation

You can deflect many inappropriate and even nasty comments by agreeing that there is some truth in the accusation and then redirecting the conversation. For example, Joe says the lesson is stupid. Instead of arguing, the teacher says, "You might be right." It is important to train yourself to hear loaded comments with the same emotion that you would feel if someone called you something neutral or silly like a "chair." This makes it much easier to think of a nonaggressive way of defusing a potential power struggle.

Answer Improbably

Imagine telling a student that you've had enough of his behavior and you offer him the option to either stop or leave. He looks you square in the eye in the middle of class and says he's not going, you can't make him stop, and concludes with "What are you going to do about it?" Imagine saying, "I'm going to finish this lesson, hop on over to the airport, and take the first flight to Mars!" How do you suppose he and the other students might react?

Behave Paradoxically

Behaving paradoxically is based on the idea that people tend to resist change when they feel forced to let go of the familiar. Think of a stubborn man who knows he drinks too much; he is likely to drink even more when nagged to stop by his concerned wife. Similarly, many of the most challenging students get lots of energy to continue their inappropriate behavior in the face of threats and punishments.

Consider the following typical and paradoxical message:

Typical: "Jane, I will tolerate no more swearing in this class. If you use those words again, you are out of here!"

Paradoxical: "Jane, you said bull____. I think you meant to say 'bull-feces.' Say it again, except this time I want to hear the proper term."

One way to think paradoxically is imagine that what the student is trying to do is acceptable, but the way she does it is inappropriate. Here are some examples:

I'm proud of you for defending yourself and stopping others from insulting you, but you can't do it by hitting. Let me show you a better way.

I'm glad you have so many wonderful things to do at home. That's great. Let's think of how to make homework one of them.

I love your energy. You are never passive or uninvolved. And your comments are really funny. I can help you use them to help other classmates laugh and learn at the same time.

> When you walk into class you always manage to get everyone to
> pay attention to you. You have fabulous presence. Can you help me
> use your gift to get others involved when I want to start the lesson?
> We can plan grand entrances together.

There are situations in which we would not advise this technique in a school setting. The most obvious is fighting or hard hitting (as opposed to the playful shoving that many middle school students use to express the combination of friendship and camaraderie).

Although a hint of humor may be appropriate, avoid sarcasm when using a paradoxical method. It works only when you convey your genuine belief that the only one with the real power to effect change is the student himself.

Use Nonverbal Messages

Students who chronically misbehave have been verbally reprimanded thousands of times before. They eventually become immune to verbal messages, which are tuned out. Try using prearranged nonverbal signals to cue students to the fact that you've had enough. It can be any mutually prearranged signal such as a facial look or a gesture.

Throw a Good Old-Fashioned Tantrum

Every so often, probably no more than two or three times a year, a well-timed tantrum in which you might yell, scream, stand on chairs, or even knock over a table or two can be wonderfully refreshing and renewing. It reminds children that you, like all humans, have your limits and that there are times you care deeply enough about your students to respond with visceral, nonviolent, but poignant, gut-releasing emotion. Although you will be reacting emotionally, be sure to throw a tantrum only when you are in control and have decided that this issue is worth it. Don't "impulsively" react this way because you are likely to say or do something you may well regret. Just remember, doing this every day makes you look like a lunatic, so be extremely selective.

Record or Videotape Your Class or Specific Students

Some students are committed to denying all responsibility for being disruptive. Furthermore, a phone call home may be greeted with a parent defending his child's actions. When you are confronted with such a situation, it can be helpful to tell the student, "Beginning today, I will be keeping the recorder on. Because I think it's important for both you and your parents to understand the problems that we have here, it will be available to your parents when we come together to discuss your school progress."

This method has been extremely effective in curtailing a wide range of inappropriate behaviors (especially verbal abuse, put-downs, and swearing). Be aware of the "cosmetic effect," however. When people first see or hear themselves, they frequently pay more attention to how they look or sound than to what they are doing. It might take three or four viewings before students can actually benefit from viewing or hearing themselves.

Focus on those students who give you the most difficulty. Discuss their feelings about the way they looked or sounded. Explore the need for change. When given a chance to actually see or hear themselves, students often gain an awareness of their negative impact and are willing to try something new. Naturally, check with administration before recording to make sure no school policies or state laws prohibit this practice.

Put Students in Charge of Their Own Problem

Because many students who misbehave are trying to feel in control, look for ways to put them in charge of moments that can be problematic. For example, students who have trouble getting from one place to the next can be put in charge of making sure everyone behaves on the way. The playground bully can be empowered to look after others to make sure there is no teasing or taunting. The student who is constantly out of her seat can be asked to plan or lead some exercises and activities for the entire class.

Use Exercise Regularly

A growing body of data suggests exercise as a treatment for ADHD; it may even be able to replace medication for some students (Wendt, 2002). In his book *Different Brains, Different Learners: How to Reach the Hard to Reach*, Jensen (2000) advocates exercise as an effective intervention with students who fit at least 5 different categories of disorders (out of 10 addressed in his book). We have become a much more interactive society that makes passive sitting and listening increasingly difficult. Introduce movement activities often in your classroom. For every 8 to 10 minutes of listening, try to think of 1 or 2 minutes of activity that requires at least some movement. This can be as simple as sharing an idea with someone, doing a "finding someone who" activity, or doing a think-pair-share.

Solicit Ideas from Colleagues

Too often in schools, we underutilize each other when it comes to borrowing potentially helpful ideas. Write out a situation or problem you face and leave off the ending—like a mystery puzzle. Distribute copies to any of the teachers in the school you trust or who you feel have a good reputation for dealing with difficult students. Include an administrator and one or two resource personnel, such as the school psychologist. Put your ego aside, if it is an issue, by also approaching teachers you silently or publicly criticize but know in your heart are more successful than you with this student population. Have each of them write in their ending or describe how they would handle the situation. Ask them to be specific.

Limitations with Chronic Students

We believe that there need to be limitations even with "unconventional" approaches. As mentioned previously, we believe that all students have a right to attend school so that their safety and security are guaranteed. Dangerous or violent behavior that includes fighting or carrying weapons cannot and must not be tolerated in a school setting. We feel strongly that dangerous behavior must be dealt with through legal channels along with school consequences that identify proper restitution required to atone for the current transgression. An acceptable action plan that specifies what the student will do differently if the situation presents itself in the future should also be expected. When necessary, an alternative setting with more support may be needed.

Working successfully with chronically misbehaving students requires a teacher who mixes democracy with authority; who is warm, caring, but also tough as nails; who responds immediately to disruptive behavior; and who is both predictably consistent and also able to remain as fair as possible. In short, working with students who chronically misbehave requires a broad repertoire of skills, an enormous amount of self-control, and a lot of support.

For the Administrator

Teachers need a lot of support when working with chronically disruptive students. Keep these points in mind to help your staff:

• **Continue to involve the parents of chronically misbehaving students.** Do not be afraid to call them at home and at work when you need to. If your teachers need an uncooperative parent to come to school, intercede when there is a problem, and use the weight of the school to get them in. If parents claim that they cannot leave work for school, tell the parents that you are sure that their child is very sorry for the inconvenience and that he or she will be waiting in the hall in 20 minutes for pickup. Keep parents of disruptive students informed of their children's progress.

• **Become an effective mediator** in the positive student confrontation method because you know both the student and teacher well.

• **Appeal directly to the families or community to assist with resolution.** If problems involving several children in a classroom might have racial or gang overtones, involving the police and social agencies can often be helpful. Communities can also help. For example, Milwaukee Public Schools has partnered with a community organization to establish "Violence-Free Zones" in some of its schools. Trained conflict mediators and troubleshooters head off trouble before it happens by closely interacting with and monitoring students known to be challenging. School climate and suspensions have been positively impacted by this approach.

• **Encourage your teachers to try new approaches.** Teachers have little to lose when trying unconventional strategies, but they often fear administrative nonsupport or disapproval. Let all your teachers know that you will support most of their plans that are nonpunitive. Ask them to share their ideas with you in advance.

• **Remember that working with difficult students is frustrating!** Please understand that when a teacher is calling a student names, is making demands of you for swift action, or is in some other way behaving "unprofessionally," this is the time for support, not debate. You can help your teachers feel less frustrated by sharing information concerning the student *and* by being a good listener who can express empathy.

• **When a student is referred to you, allow at least 15 minutes to pass before returning the student to the classroom.** If possible, accompany the student back to class.

• **Address teachers' common belief that administrators aren't tough enough.** Early in the school year, let staff know you expect them to deal with most issues regarding discipline; but when they send you a student, you will do your very best to fix the problem. However, remind them that challenging students are not so easy to fix, and your goal is at least to send them back a better-behaved student for a longer period of time. Be open and invite them to join you in brainstorming other possibilities if that sort of collaboration does not happen regularly, but let them know that when they put the student in your hands, you plan to do things your way.

• **Put your teachers in a position to succeed.** Teachers do better with difficult students when they are teaching within their own strengths. Avoid having one teacher responsible for teaching all subjects to a self-contained class. Instead, allow a teacher who prefers English and math to teach those two subjects to two classes while another teaches social studies and science.

9

Teaching Strategies and Classroom Setup

❧ WHAT WE HAVE LEARNED ❧

Due to a convergence of two unrelated simultaneous events—(1) the writing of this book and (2) one of the authors having a total knee replacement—we have new insights to add to this chapter. The surgery included great pain, the relearning of simple daily tasks like sitting up, and lots of support. Four main themes emerged during the hospital and rehabilitation stay:

• **Pain understands pain.** The more pain we feel, the more we empathize with the pain of others. When teaching lessons, it is important for teachers to remember a time when learning something was hard for them. This will help teachers treat struggling students humanely and with dignity.

• **It is very difficult to tell how hard any given task is for another person.** What might seem easy for most is sometimes very difficult for some. We must never assume any given learning assignment is easy for every student. It helps to always assume that learning difficulties are real, even when they seem extreme.

• **People who are struggling to learn what might appear to be even simple tasks need lots of support and encouragement, but not manipulation.** When struggling with rehabilitation, it was important to hear encouragement. However, an hourly or daily reward was not necessary. We believe the same is true for children. They need assurance that they are making progress, are on the right track, and should be proud of what they have accomplished so far. Such assurance can usually be achieved without the added use of manipulation.

• **Every person learns at his or her own rate of speed.** Some learn faster than others. Speed is neither a sufficient nor desirable criterion for success. Like baseball, school and learning are long seasons. As often as possible, allow students to go at their own pace.

Great teachers understand that great lessons are the great equalizer. The better the lesson is, the less likely students are to disrupt it. Great teaching means being successful with all students, regardless of ability, special needs, or cultural variations. Yet this challenge has become greater than ever with general education teachers being expected to teach special education students with very little if any prior training. Special educators are asked to hop from class to class, often frustrated by not being able to fully immerse themselves in the curriculum.

At the same time, society increasingly values instant gratification. Cell phones, instant messaging, text messaging, e-mail, and video games consume the minds, thoughts, and feelings of our youth. The challenge for teachers is to make lessons more stimulating, exciting, entertaining, and gratifying than the very things that distract students from succeeding in school. This chapter explores how. Finally, when our lessons are occasionally lacking, we can compete by giving students what technology cannot: interaction, affection, dialogue, and connections with real humans, to name a few.

Motivated students cause fewer discipline problems. Enthusiastic teachers who present their material in stimulating, meaningful ways and treat students with respect and dignity almost always have fewer behavior problems than those who do not. When students are actively learning content that they can personally relate to, they usually have neither the time nor energy to create discipline problems. Conversely, when students feel that they are passive receptacles for irrelevant knowledge, they become bored, turn off, and find satisfaction in acting out.

Try telling your class early in the school year:

Class, I need to let you all know right now that I will always do my best never to waste your time this year. I hate when people waste mine, and I will try hard not to waste yours. This means I will do my best to give you work you can do to get better today than you were yesterday. I will not give you homework just so you will not be playing video games or watching television at night. You might not like all the assignments I give, and you might not understand why I'm giving each, but remember, I promise to do my best never to waste your time this year.

It is also important that the teacher dictates the pace of the class. The teacher decides on the attitude he or she comes to work with. It is easy to picture a difficult student as a rude, nasty, defiant, disruptive pain. Try to reframe these views into more positive ones. Instead of thinking about that child as rude, think of him as outspoken. Instead of thinking about her as lazy or unmotivated, think of her as calm or relaxed. You have incredible power to decide how to picture your students before they enter your room. No one can take this power away from you.

The Art of Assigning Homework

We've already suggested telling your class that you will do your best never to waste their time this year. This announcement goes a long way in getting homework finished. If students have homework in all five subjects, but you've already said you aren't going to waste time, there is a good chance they will start with yours. Here are a few more helpful homework tips.

Allow students to have a say in which nights they'd prefer homework. Say something like this:

Class, I will be giving homework two or three nights per week this year. Many teachers think they are being nice by giving homework all week and none on Fridays. I'm not saying I won't do that, but I want to give you a choice. I know that many of you are tired when you get home. You've been in school all day. Some of you have sports practice at night or some type of music event. I know many of your parents work during the week and are tired themselves at night.

If you have a parent who travels for work or works late, they might not be home to help. So you decide. Would you prefer three nights Monday through Thursday or one night Monday through Thursday and a bit more on Fridays?

Let's say the students select Tuesday and Friday. That decision helps structure the lives of their parents, too. At parent night you can say:

> Mr. and Mrs. Parent, I just want to let you know how my class works this year. I promise to do my best not to waste your or your child's time. This means I won't be giving homework every night. In this class it will be on Tuesdays and Fridays. Please set aside at least one hour every Tuesday night to work with your son or daughter. If they come home on Tuesdays and say they don't have homework, probably they're misinforming you. If you want to put them in a sports league or have them take music lessons, please do it on a night other than Tuesday.

Parents will love you for this. It keeps them from having to constantly nag their son or daughter about homework. Some parents will say, "Why are you giving my child homework on Fridays?" You can respond, "I don't know. Ask your child. The class picked Tuesdays and Fridays."

This approach also gives the teacher more leverage when the homework is not done. Let's say a student comes unprepared on Monday morning. It is now so much easier to say something like this:

Teacher: The homework isn't done? I'm disappointed that you did not follow through on your decision. I guess from now on I'll decide which nights you get homework.
Student: No, we can make decisions.
Teacher: Good, you have one more chance. I do not want to hear any stories about why the work isn't done from now on.

Homework is a topic that leads to many power struggles and unmotivated students.

Teacher: Do problems 1 through 10.
Child: I do not want to do 10 problems.

And an argument ensues. But if the teacher cares only about the outcome of the homework, this request becomes much easier to handle.

Teacher: Do problems 1 through10.
Child: I do not want to do 10 problems.
Teacher: OK, that's fine. How many do you want to do?
Child: None.
Teacher: None is not an option. But I can live with five. In fact, you decide which five will best show me you understand the material. Or you can do the five easiest! You decide.

Like a good consequence, homework may be viewed as a vehicle to a destination. The destination is not negotiable. The student will learn how to multiply. The student will learn how to read. The student's writing will improve. Multiplication, reading, and writing are the destinations. Stop caring so much about the vehicle. If one student needs to do 10 problems and another needs to do 5, that's fine. But make sure you make it very clear that "You will show me you know how to multiply!"

Relate Content and Homework to the Individual

Many times students will ask a teacher why they have to do something—for example, "Why do I have to do this assignment?" or "What's the point of this quiz?" Most teachers answer with the classic "Because I said so" or "Because it's going to be on your quiz." They are answering a question with a statement. Instead, a much better response to the question "Why do I have to?" is to answer with a question:

Student: I do not want to do this stupid assignment. Why do I have to?
Teacher: Well, what do you want to be when you grow up?

This is a great answer for any grade level. With an elementary student, it is "Well, what do you want to be when you grow up?" With a high school student, it might be "Well, what are you going to do when you get out of here?" Either way, the response gets the student to internalize and gives the teacher time to relate the content to the student's interest.

Student: A professional baseball player.
Teacher: You want to be a ball player? I think that's great. I bet you want to be on TV and make all that money that the best players make.
Student: Yeah.
Teacher: And did you know that if you play for the Yankees and live in New York, you are going to have to pay these things called taxes?
Student: So?
Teacher: So? So New York State is going to take more than 7 percent of your paycheck. And if you have no clue how to calculate percents, you'll have no way of knowing if the state is taking out more than they should! So of course you need to know how to calculate percents. I'll see your math homework tomorrow. When you're playing shortstop for the Yankees, I want you to be able to keep all of your money!

Answering a question with a question will buy you time to think of a good answer. If you still do not have good answers, simply ask another question: "Really? Why do you want to be a professional ballplayer?" Or, "If that doesn't work out, what else might you want to do?"

Occasionally a student will say, "I don't know." Here's one way to handle that response:

Student: I'm not doing the homework. Why do I have to?
Teacher: Well, what do you want to be when you grow up?
Student: I don't know.
Teacher: Well, if you did know, what would you say?
Student: I said I don't know.
Teacher: OK. Well, I know you love video games. Did you know that the video game industry is one of the fastest-growing industries in the country?
Student: No.
Teacher: Well, it is. And I bet you'd love working for a company that writes and produces video games. Wouldn't that be a fun job?
Student: I guess.
Teacher: You guess? Because I'll tell you this: There are a lot of people just like you who would love a job like that. And if you can't write basic paragraphs on a job application, you won't even get an interview! I look forward to seeing your writing improvements tomorrow, just so you can be around video games for the rest of your life!

Sometimes relating motivation to the future will not work because some students live entirely in the present. For them the future is too conceptual and far away. Here are other possible answers with such students:

"Because this assignment will be fun" (if it is).

"Because it takes courage to try something you do not like. I wonder how brave you are?"

"If you really do not like this assignment, do a different one that shows me you can write a good essay."

Here are a few other things to keep in mind when assigning homework.

- **Be sure the homework is challenging but not overwhelming.** Homework should be the right length and intensity. It should not be assigned to fill time but to complete a learning objective.
- **Make the homework as interesting as possible.** Students do not need to love every assignment, and drill and practice certainly can be used as homework. But remember, homework competes with the Internet, phone, iPod, television, sleep, friends, and family.
- **Relate the assignment to what was covered in class.** Homework that is not integrated into class activities is perceived by students as a waste of time. We already promised not to waste their time. Simply going over the homework in class is not enough. The learning gained by doing the homework should directly relate to other class activities.
- **Correct and go over it quickly.** When homework is returned weeks after it was handed in, it is of little value to the students' learning. Homework can be returned faster if it is self-corrected. Try to give homework back as soon as possible so true learning can occur from it. Homework should not be corrected by peers because doing so makes each student's performance known to others and therefore a possible source of embarrassment.
- **Give choices.** Students are more receptive to assignments that offer some selection. If there are 12 questions at the end of a chapter, tell them to do the 6 they like most. Most will even look at all 12 in order to pick their 6 favorites. The biggest benefit of choice is 50 percent less grading for you. For some of us, that is the equivalent of a second life. The process of selection may be of more learning benefit than answering the questions.

Four Characteristics of Motivating Lessons

These principles and examples come from *Motivating Students Left Behind: Practical Strategies for Reaching and Teaching Your Most Difficult Students* (Curwin, 2006).

Get Students to Recognize and Use Familiar Stimuli

When teaching something new, use television, movies, advertisements and songs, or have students create one of these to demonstrate their knowledge. Here is an example of using song.

Divide the class into small groups, and ask each group to make a list of the members' favorite songs. Ask them to connect in some way the song title with the topic to be learned. Here's an example from an astronomy lesson:

Student Songs*

- "Stairway to Heaven"
- "I Can See for Miles"
- "The Night Has a Thousand Eyes"
- "Blinded by the Light"
- "So Far Away"
- "I'll Follow the Sun"

Another way to do this activity is to tell the students in advance what the topic is and have them think of songs to match. Here are examples:

- "Every Breath You Take"—Biology
- "Purple Haze"—Art
- "Born in the U.S.A."—Social Studies
- "Running on Empty"—Driver Education

---

*The authors made a difficult decision on which song titles to use in these examples. Should we use songs familiar to ourselves and most teachers or songs familiar to most students? We chose the former because the music of students is so diverse, we think it is best for teachers to use songs that specifically relate to their own students. In addition, our youthfulness notwithstanding, these are the song titles we know best.

- "Wish You Were Here"—Geography
- "What's Going On?"—Current Events, Environmental Studies
- "Three Times a Lady"—Math
- "The Way We Were"—History

Most students nowadays are likely to choose rap or country music, which is fine for this purpose.

Ask Compelling Questions

Great questions drive great lessons. Have you ever forgotten the name of a song and made yourself crazy trying to remember it? Great questions create the same feeling in students. Here is a sample from various content areas that teachers have shared with us.

Middle School Math
Question: What does Martin Luther King have in common with algebra?
Answer: Both are concerned with equality.

High School Grammar
Question: Do nouns have sex?
Answer: Yes, that's where plurals come from.

1st Grade Science Class Studying Particles
Question: What is the smallest thing you ever held in your hand?
Answer (Solicit answers from your students.)

Upper-Level Study of the Pilgrims
Question: Is there anything your parents could ever do to you that would make you run away from home?

Encourage Guessing

Most school subjects have their own name for guessing. Math uses *estimating*, science uses *hypothesizing*, and literature uses *foreshadowing.* Once students have guessed, they naturally want to know if they are correct. Have you ever taken a magazine quiz and not looked at the upside-down answers to compare them with your own? Learning happens when students check their answers with the correct ones.

Use Challenge

Challenge is a universal motivator when context and level are considered. *Context* means that the student cares about the subject. Students who do not care about math are harder to motivate than students who do. Even more important is *level*. The challenge must not be too easy or too hard. If the degree of difficulty is at the right level, even those not particularly interested in the content are more likely to be motivated. A student who is not interested in math will be likely to do math problems if she believes she can succeed with the first one she sees.

Changing Student Attitudes Toward Learning

Many of us have had the experience of expecting a required class to be a horrible experience, only to find it was really pleasant. Here are three ways that teachers can change negative attitudes toward learning:

• **What you teach makes students better at something they care about.** Most people want to get better at what they love. Take time at the beginning of the year to find out what students love to do, and include their interests in the lessons.

• **Make success possible throughout the instructional sequences.** Most negative attitudes have their roots in a long-term history of failure. Try to make it impossible for students to fail if they truly make an effort.

• **Demonstrate a love and passion for what you teach.** The athletes and entertainers we enjoy most are the ones who love what they do. It shows by the passion and energy they demonstrate. If you merely go through the motions, don't be surprised if your students do the same. Try to teach at least one thing that excites you every day. It does not have to relate directly to the curriculum.

Evaluation and Grading

If truly attempting to motivate individual students, then it is best to compare their work and behavior with their previous work and behavior. Imagine you come to work every day and do the best job you know how to do. On your way out, the principal hands you a grade of *D* or *F*. When you ask why the low grade, the following conversation occurs:

Principal: Yeah, you worked hard. But your teaching is not as good as the lady down the hall.
Teacher: I know. But she's been here for 20 years, and I've been here for 2 months.
Principal: I know. But you are both 4th grade teachers. And we compare 4th grade teachers with each other here. Maybe someday you'll be as good as her.

This conversation is ridiculous—no decent administrator would say these things. Yet in the classroom this type of situation happens all the time. And we wonder why students who don't measure up give up?

Here is an example of how grading can destroy motivation: "Kristie's paper is an *A*, which means Freddie's paper must be a *C* because it's not as good as Kristie's." With this mind-set, Freddie learns he has no chance of ever getting an *A* because he isn't as good as Kristie and probably never will be.

When people in any profession learn that their best work or effort is not good enough, they have two options. Most give up and quit—the first option. When a baseball player can't hit a fastball anymore, he retires or walks away from the game. Students can't walk away from 2nd grade. So they stay and disrupt. Then when failing, at least they can say, "Yeah, but I didn't even try."

The second option is to cheat. Some sports players chose this option. Their best wasn't good enough so they took steroids or performance-enhancing drugs. Some students will choose to cheat. The thought is "I need a 90 average to make honor roll. I know I can't get a 90 myself, so let me copy someone who can." At least cheaters want to stay in the game.

A technique to combat these two options is to change the goal so that students change their behavior. Challenge them to compete with themselves. Here is an example of a teacher who did this and saw tremendous success.

Mr. Lester taught an 8th grade class of emotionally disturbed students. These students rarely received grades higher than a *C*, and most of their averages were closer to *D+*. For the first quarter of the school year, Mr. Lester decided to give every student an *A* on his or her first assignment no matter what that assignment looked like. Without telling the students, *he decided that of the first five grades of the quarter, none would be lower than a* B. Mr. Lester's goal was to see if the higher grades would make the students feel as if they had something to lose. Many disruptive, unmotivated, and unproductive students have been taught to hold tight to what they have. This is the reason most won't take off their headphones, hats, and jackets. No one buys them a new one if it gets stolen or lost. Mr. Lester took the same approach with grades. He also had nothing to lose. "They were already doing poorly, so why not try something different?" he told us.

Mr. Lester began the second quarter by telling the students that they could all maintain their *A*s or *B*s by improving their individual performance. This message was repeated the two next quarters, but the work that Mr. Lester required increased each time. Most students tried hard to keep their good grades, a prize they had never known before.

Once students feel that a good grade is achievable, many have a lot more energy to maintain, even if it means more work. A system of evaluation that either forces students to compete with each other or maintains the same criteria for all students despite intellectual and academic differences is destined to produce winners and losers. The losers, more often than not, are tomorrow's discipline problems. They have learned that if they work hard, are well motivated, and do their best, they are rewarded with a *C* or *D*. Few of us can do our best for very long with such minimal validation. What Mr. Lester did with his class will be completely impossible if you care more about grades than you do about learning.

Evaluation is an important link between behavior and learning. The point of evaluation is to give students information that can be used for self-understanding and improved learning.

Involving Students in the Evaluation Process

A key to having evaluation contribute to hope and belief in success is to involve students in the process. Here are a few important ways:

• Elicit test questions from students.

• Allow students to choose how many questions a test or quiz should have.

• Incorporate student ideas as to what information should be on the test.

• Have students test each other. This is usually done more for practice. Because of the importance of privacy, students also should not see the grade of another student.

• Allow students to substitute a few questions on a test with others they feel more confident answering on the same subject.

• Consider including in your grading policy a new set of three Rs: redo, retake, and revise. Allow students to improve their grade through one or more of these means. To keep things manageable, you might set time limits (e.g., "You have three days to improve your essay"). Be sure to tell them you will figure out their new grade after the makeup work is complete.

• Occasionally allow students to grade themselves, especially on assignments requiring creativity and without a right or wrong answer. Base the criteria on a rubric or outline you've presented prior to the assignment.

Competition: Is It a Good Thing in the Classroom?

Not usually. When students are forced to compete with each other, they often start to dislike their classmates. If a few students always win and a few others always lose, the students who lose begin disliking those who win. This situation can lead to bullying and aggression. When a school has class rankings, someone is ranked first, which means someone else is ranked last. Students ranked at the bottom feel lousy about school. Their motivation to learn sharply decreases, and they often give up or drop out. Competition between students also forces them to stop pushing themselves to get better. If students are competing for the top spot in the class, one might decide not to take an advanced placement class for fear of a lower grade and a loss of a ranking. Some students stop helping each other because they do not want one of their classmates to take their spot. Some students will actually give each other wrong information if the competition gets too intense.

Advocates of competition in the classroom claim it is highly stimulating and motivates students to achieve their best. The strongest argument is that competition is a fact of life. Students will be unprepared for the real world if they do not experience competition in school. Although we are advocates for getting students ready for the real world, unlike in school, in life people get to pick the profession or field they want to compete in. School is better suited for preparing students for life by getting them to believe in themselves, which is accomplished by experiencing success following real effort.

Motivation can be boosted through "voluntary competition." This term is simple to understand: is the activity or event chosen by the participant without undue pressure or indirect coercion by the teacher, parent, or other students? With voluntary competition, the student understands the situation before the competition. When a student understands there are only 15 spots on the basketball team and tries out anyway, she knows going in that getting cut is a possibility. When a student chooses to enter an essay into a competition knowing he might not win but is excited by the prospect of seeing how he compares with others, he might become more motivated to write. When students enroll in an advanced placement class and know that a lot of study will be needed to achieve a 4 or 5 on the test, that insight could help them set high goals that can inspire motivation. Just be sure the student knows the possible outcomes before the competition begins.

Making Inclusion Work Best

The term *inclusion* has become almost as popular as *detention* in most schools. The general concept is that special education students are placed in general education classes. We have found the best inclusion classrooms have a special education teacher and a general education teacher in the room as full partners for all or at least half of the day, which is not currently the most popular model. They truly become coteachers and are able to learn from each other.

The special education teacher becomes a content expert by working with the same general education teacher all day, every day, and can then better apply special techniques or adaptations within a more thorough understanding of the content. Modifying assignments, tests, and quizzes because they are in the room all the time and have a solid handle on the content becomes much easier, gaining much benefit for the special education students.

The general education teacher learns new, exciting, cutting-edge strategies and ideas for working with special needs students. The general education students benefit because they have two teachers in the room full-time who can help, and the special needs students benefit because their strengths are more likely to be tapped.

If one of the teachers gets sick or needs time off, the class actually moves forward because the other teacher is still there and knows the routines, plans, content, and, most important, the students.

For inclusion to be most effective, it is so important for both teachers to be seen and viewed as *equals*. Both names should be on the door. Each teacher should be introduced as "a 5th grade teacher." Or, "This year you actually have two English teachers. Isn't that great?" This practice eliminates the stigma that so often comes when a regular education student asks a special education teacher for help. Naturally, each teacher knows and assumes his or her individual role. For inclusion to work best, the teachers must trust each other completely. The general education teacher has to trust that the special education teacher knows how to modify assignments, grades, quizzes, and tests. The special education teacher needs to trust that the general education teacher knows how to plan lessons, understands the content, and will challenge students to improve. At the end of the day, there needs to be an understanding that the special education teacher is responsible for students with IEPs and the general education teacher is responsible for everyone else.

Making Group Work Fantastic

Group work can be either phenomenal or horrendous. Here is a step-by-step guide to making group work effective in your classroom.

1. Put students in groups yourself rather than letting them do so. Students tend to choose to work with the same people if left to decide on their own. There are many other places for students to choose. This isn't one of them.

2. Make a "no complaints allowed" announcement. Tell your class before the first time you ever do group work, "Class, some of you are going to complain about who you are working with. You may tell me you do not like that person and do not want to work with them. I just want to tell you right now if I ever hear you complain about who you are working with, you will be guaranteed to work with that person every single day until you complete a task together without complaining!"

3. Limit groups to five students. We prefer to have six groups of five instead of five groups of six.

4. After students are placed in group, tell them the two T's: time and task. Tell them how many minutes they have to complete the assignment first, and then make them repeat it. For example: "You will have eight minutes to get this done. How many minutes will you have?" When some students can't remember how much time they have, someone else will remind them. Then tell them the task or the assignment.

5. Remember that it is always easier to give than it is to take things away. This is why it is better to give less time than you think an activity is going to take. If you think the assignment will take 10 minutes, tell the class they have 5. If you think 20 minutes will do, tell the class they have 14. By giving less time, you create a sense of urgency. If students finish quickly, you can bring the group back. If they are not finished after the 14 minutes, you can always extend time, usually without telling them. If you try taking time away from students, look out. "You said we had 10 minutes and it's only been 7!" You do not need to hear this complaint.

6. After you tell them the two T's, number each student 1 through 5. Each number corresponds with a specific job for that assignment.

7. Make sure your number 1s are always the group leaders. This is the most important role and the one most teachers forget. The group leaders have no other responsibility than to lead the group. Their job is to make sure everyone else is doing the job they are supposed to do and then to help students who might struggle with their roles. Make your most disruptive or your smartest students the group leaders first.

8. Assign the rest of the roles. Number 2s are the readers. Number 3s are the note takers. Number 4s organize the notes so that number 5s can present the information to the class. Now all students must work together to complete the task.

9. Tell the group members to follow their leaders. Tell your class the following: "During group time, you are only allowed to talk to the teacher if you are a group leader. If you are having a problem with your role or are unclear about the directions, you need to go to your group leader first. If they can't help, they will come to me." Instead of worrying about 30 students, the teacher has to worry only about 6. Those students are responsible for everyone else in their group.

10. Give each group leader a red cup and a green cup to signal the groups' progress. Red means stop; green means go. The teacher hangs back and watches the room. If you see green cups all around, it means the groups are working well. If you see a red cup, go directly to the group leader and ask what the problem is. This system allows the teacher to spend as much time as necessary with an individual group without worrying about the other groups.

There is nothing more annoying than a teacher coming over every five minutes to ask if things are OK. Like a great waiter who can read a customer's nod quickly and refill his glass, red cup/green cup lets you know quickly when you are needed. Naturally, there is no substitute for your judgment. Like the great waiter who comes by occasionally to make sure all is well, touch base occasionally with each group to be sure they are functioning properly.

11. Reconsider switching group roles. Do we always switch roles? The answer used to be a definitive yes. That is not the case anymore. For example, we have found that displaying leadership skills or being well organized is something that many people naturally possess. It is best during group time to put people in roles that fit them best. The Chicago Bulls didn't move Michael Jordan from guard to center just to change it up. The one role we think everyone needs is that of public speaker, because presenting your ideas in a public forum or on a job interview is an important life skill that is rarely taught in school.

Think of group work as a business. The teacher is the CEO. Your name is on the door. But any good business also has a director of sales and marketing, a director of human resources, and a director of public relations. There needs to be a special reason for a regular salesperson to go directly to the CEO. The CEO usually says, "Ask your manager first before you come to me."

These steps can initially be a lot of work, but your students will quickly learn how to gain maximum benefit from working in groups.

Teaching Effectively in a Block Schedule

Teaching in a block format can be difficult. It is not easy sustaining the attention of students for 40 minutes, let alone 80. It is best to break your block into four different mini-lessons. For example, if teaching English, you might do 20 minutes of poetry, 20 minutes of reading, 20 minutes of writing, and 20 minutes of public speaking. If a student hates poetry or a different part of the lesson, he knows it only lasts for 20 minutes. Do not do one thing for the entire 60 to 80 minutes. Even if a student loves the activity, eventually satiation leads to boredom.

With block scheduling come longer changing times between classes. Most 60- to 80-minute blocks have 6- to 8-minute changing times. This also is a good thing. Students have a chance to go to the bathroom, get a quick snack, talk to their friends, and still get to class on time.

The only downside to blocks is that teachers need to plan for a longer amount of time. Some teachers claim students do not retain as much information when they do not review every day. This is a valid concern. However, block scheduling allows significant time for review directly after a lesson is taught.

Fostering Creativity in the Classroom

Classroom activities that foster creativity are almost always highly motivating. Many units are devoted especially to the development of creativity, such as problem solving, dramatics, and creative writing. The following questions can be used to review any lesson to see if it fosters creativity.

1. How many times were students asked to respond to something that had more than one right answer?

2. In what circumstances were students required to deal with more than one possibility?

3. What activities required students to defer judgment?

4. How many activities actually required students to get out of their seat to talk to someone else in order to complete a task?

5. How often were guessing and hypothesizing encouraged?

6. In what situations were students encouraged to try the unknown and take reasonable risks without fear of failure or punishment?

7. In what ways were students encouraged to think of new ideas?

8. In what ways were all of the senses used in the lesson?

9. How is student creativity visibly apparent in the classroom?

10. How often do you ask students to find similarities in seemingly unrelated issues, events, or items?

Teaching with Technology

Type "The Great Depression" on Google, and you will find enough information to complete a 5,000-page research paper. Technology has made gathering information much easier. It has also made cheating much easier. Numerous Web sites sell research papers. Some students copy and paste articles they find online and pass them off as their own. Teachers need to be out in front of students. Tell them before the assignment that you will check the Internet if a paper looks suspicious.

Most kids love computers, and schools can buy hundreds of good programs to help foster learning and creativity. Be sure to set limits with the use of technology. In an elementary room, 45 minutes (total) is a good guideline for time spent on the computer. In a middle or high school, the teacher has more discretion. Be sure your school has a strong filter that blocks inappropriate Web sites and any site a student is spending too much time on. The teacher should be the only person with the password.

For some students, computers have made a major difference in their behavior. A teacher in a training session on discipline recently announced proudly, "Last year I had so many discipline problems that I almost quit teaching. This year I have none." When asked how she made such a remarkable change, she replied, "Last year I taught math. This year, I am teaching computers."

It is important to understand that technology can help create lessons that could never be taught otherwise. It can increase motivation, stimulation, and participation. It can teach mastery learning or provide individual instruction with special tutorials for each step of the lesson. When using technology as part of the instructional process, carefully consider the following points:

- **Technology excels at providing information.** Teachers need to instruct students in how to process that information and how to make decisions based on it. Many Web sites have incorrect or politically motivated information. Mrs. Erin Brandvold, a teacher from the Empowerment School in Hayward, California, shows her class a Web site that looks authentic but really has a hidden racist agenda. She then instructs students what to look for when accessing information.

• **Certain technologies, such as computer workstations, are often used by a single student.** Extensive isolation is not healthy for children who need social interaction and communication as part of their educational experience. Cooperative learning strategies can easily be adapted to incorporate computers.

• **Students are media saturated at home.** We have already mentioned the vast number of hours children spend watching television. Many children spend much of their free time playing computer and video games. We must be careful to provide students a balanced diet of instructional activities.

• **Technology can teach students to be passive.** Active learning is essential to the full development of the child.

For the Administrator

Teachers must have administrative support before innovation can occur, but support alone is not sufficient. Teachers need concrete ideas and examples of what can be done to help difficult students. They need time built into their day to develop ideas and create dynamic and meaningful lessons. Most important, they need to feel safe so that they can learn from their failures and successes without fear of administrative ridicule or penalty.

Although it is good to have goals and standards, test pressure often leads to impatience, frustration with slow learners, and a general feeling of anxiety among the staff. Even more harmful is the notion that all teachers must be at the same place in the curriculum at the same time. If you want higher scores, less referrals, safer conditions, and more effective results, lower the temperature for test results. Let your teachers teach, meet individual needs, and take the time to deal with behavior problems when they are small. Paradoxically, less time worrying about the test and more time teaching invariably lead to better test scores.

Because boredom is a major cause of classroom disruption, we suggest that you closely examine the curriculum. Update it so that it is relevant and focuses attention on more than memorizing the facts. If the curriculum is boring to adults, it will most likely be boring to students.

We ask you to examine your evaluation systems and consider alternate ways of reporting student progress. Try to use methods that describe strengths and areas for improvement without judging them. All students should be able to achieve success if they expend effort. Minimize competition that pits student against student and find as many ways as possible to encourage cooperation. When competition does exist, see that it is voluntary and focuses primarily on learning rather than on winning. Ask your teachers to get students to compete against themselves and be sure to find a way of valuing effort at least as much as outcomes.

Be sure to have teachers work in teams. Teams can be made up of faculty members who teach the same subject. This way meetings are spent discussing teaching strategies and ideas rather than complaining about difficult students. This approach will also minimize teacher boredom as the team learns to trust each other and share methods, ideas, and lessons with each other. Help them learn how to observe each other nonjudgmentally so that they may look to each other for inspirational support before the going gets rough. Create a climate where all teachers feel comfortable sharing ideas, thoughts, and opinions. Get rid of the subculture that exists in so many schools that says, "The longer you've been here, the more you must know." Emphasize the importance to teachers of how varying one's process of teaching and methods of instruction can positively affect discipline problems in the classroom.

10

Special Problems

 WHAT WE HAVE LEARNED

Times change, and so do the problems we are most concerned about. In this edition's final chapter, we address three main issues: the prevalence of special needs students in regular education settings, challenges in working with difficult parents, and ways to help students in high-poverty urban areas where achievement and behavior remain particularly stubborn problems.

Since the first edition, disorders that were not even identified have become prevalent. The Individuals with Disabilities Education Act (IDEA) now provides specific guidelines about what can and cannot be done to discipline special education students. The U.S. Centers for Disease Control and Prevention (2007) estimate that one in 150 children has an autism-spectrum disorder. Although attention deficit hyperactivity disorder (ADHD) has been known for decades, an ever-growing number of students are being diagnosed. Medication can be of benefit behaviorally (Fabiano et al., 2007) and possibly academically, but some studies show little if any improved achievement (MTA Cooperative Group, 2004). We will explore both attitudinal concerns and helpful classroom interventions for these increasingly prevalent disorders.

We address two other special problems in this chapter: interacting with difficult parents and teaching youth in urban areas. More and more teachers and administrators have identified concerns in working with belligerent and enabling parents who either create behavior problems in their children or add fuel to the fire. Schools serving impoverished youth, largely concentrated in urban areas, have special problems and concerns unique to them. This chapter offers practical solutions to addressing these challenges.

Students with Special Needs

We recently met a teacher who complained about a 2nd grade student who didn't pay attention. When asked for an example, she replied, "When he ties his shoe, he knocks everything off his desk. By the time he picks everything up, his shoe is untied again, and it starts all over. He hums in a low tone and occasionally cruises around the room." When asked if he had the correct answer when called upon, she answered, "He always knows the right answer." The real problem, then, was that he paid attention but in a disturbing way.

Most ADHD students have a particularly hard time concentrating on things that don't interest them. Many are "burdened" by a bright mind that doesn't slow down. School is especially challenging due to its lock-step approach. These students often grow up into adults adept at inventing or at participating in creative new ventures where lots of simultaneous ideas lead to breakthroughs. When young, however, they usually find the "sit quietly, pay attention, raise your hand" mentality that most schools require especially difficult.

Because the spectrum of autistic disorders ranges from intellectually gifted to severely limited, it is impossible to offer a one-size-fits-all set of solutions. Many students with autism have sensory issues leading to hypersensitive reactions to touch, sound, or sight. Most become extremely focused on something to the exclusion of everything else. Interrupting this focus can be unsettling and lead to anxiety or anger. Many have difficulty correctly reading their immediate social circumstances, which often causes them to misinterpret other people's words or body language. Without support, they can be easy targets for bullies.

Several strategies offered in Chapter 8 are appropriate for students with these needs, such as integrating exercise throughout the day and teaching students better self-control. Whenever possible, these strategies should be offered as suggestions that leave room for the student to give input as well.

Classroom Management Strategies for Students with Excessive Energy

Many regular education students also benefit from these ideas, but they are particularly appropriate for students with excess energy. The next section describes strategies that are oriented more toward students with communication or social issues.

• *Velcro.* Glue or tape a two-inch strip of Velcro underneath a student's desk or chair with the rough side accessible. Suggest to the student that when the need to get out of her seat arises, she should first rub the Velcro. The stimulation of movement is usually all a student is seeking, and rubbing the Velcro often helps fill this need.

• *Use of keyboards.* Students who have trouble writing things by hand are often more productive at a keyboard. Simply reduce handwriting requirements by giving them the opportunity to do their work on computers, both at home and in class.

• *Swimming noodles.* Have you ever seen the long Styrofoam noodles children use to float with in the pool? Slice a noodle into three sections (one noodle works for three different students). Place a section at the feet of students who move their legs a lot, and allow them to roll it back and forth. Because the noodle is Styrofoam, it doesn't make any noise when rolled.

• *Portable office.* Our dear friend Marylin Applebaum, of Applebaum Associates, suggests making a "portable office" to help distractible students. Simply take two file folders to create a three-sided screen for the student's desktop. The student now has a comfortable work area that blocks distractions.

• *Music stands.* For students who prefer standing, place a few music stands around the perimeter of your classroom and let students do assignments while standing. This is a great strategy because the music stands are adjustable and have a hard, smooth surface that allows students to write while standing.

• *Two desks.* For students who can't sit still for an extended time, assign them two desks in different areas of the room, and allow movement from desk to desk depending on time or task. For example, say, "Do the first two problems at this desk before going to your other desk." The next day you might have the student try three problems before moving.

• *Controlled territory.* For elementary students, use masking tape to make a square (or some other familiar shape) around their desks. This becomes their personal "roaming space." The idea is to enlarge the area they can move in. Tell the student, "If you need to get up and move, that's fine. Just stay inside your area. I trust you won't disturb anyone else." Make the area big enough so that the student has room to roam but small enough to limit distractions.

• *Superorganizational structures.* Disorganization and disruption often go hand in hand. Many students who struggle continually lose and forget their things. Papers and notes are often disorganized and unmanageable. Notebooks are typically stuffed with papers from three or four different subjects. Superorganizers can help. Provide boxes (cigar boxes are perfect—let the students decorate the outsides), multicolored folders, and binders for each subject. When it's time to change classes or subjects, the completed work is placed in its own storage holder. Students often need considerable practice putting the right item in the correct location. Find a special place in the room for storage of the organizers. It is also helpful to assign a well-organized student to coach a disorganized "buddy." The organized one can help make sure the disorganized peer has the proper materials and places papers in the correct file or folder.

• *Self-monitoring devices.* Many students with impulse control issues have trouble monitoring their own behavior. One solution is to temporarily provide an external monitor. If a student frequently blurts out in class, it's OK to choose a reasonable amount of blurts for a given time period. The number should be (1) within reach of the student's ability, (2) workable for you, and (3) reasonable for other students. Give the student markers for blurts to keep track of the number. Markers can include cards, pieces of tape, or a form of tokens (not candy or money). It is best for students to monitor the markers, but if they need help, take one away privately each time a student blurts. When the markers are gone, the student has no more blurts for that time period. Adjust the number of markers up or down if necessary. The long-term goal is to fade out the use of markers as the student improves monitoring his own behavior.

• *Seat placement.* Distractible students are not usually at their best in either rear or front seats. Rear seats are too far from the teacher, and front seats give their distractions center stage for all to see. The best placement is on the wings. You might say, "Amal, I'd like to change your seat because I think it will help you to concentrate better. Are you OK with that, or do you think there's an even better seat that will help you get your work done?"

• *Things to tap on.* Tapping pencils (or other similar objects) drives us all crazy, but it's not the movement that does it—it's the noise. Tapping on sponges, piles of tissue paper, carpeting, or old mouse pads will do. Remove the noise, and would-be drummers can beat away without distracting others.

• *Time to wander.* Make movement a legitimate part of students' day. When you notice restlessness creeping in, ask if they would like a drink or if they need to use the restroom. It is important for some students to be given time to work out of their seats during class. This can also be a good time to send a restless student on an errand. We know a teacher who asked a student to check all the water fountains to see how many needed repair.

Additional strategies to help student with ADHD or Autism

• *Establish predictable routines especially during transitions.* Many students with ADHD or autism do best when the environment is orderly and predictable. Try to avoid surprises. For example, it is usually best to avoid pop quizzes, unpredictable assignments, or unplanned activities. When the student is involved in an assignment or project, avoid interruptions such as initiating spontaneous conversation. When interrupted, some students will completely ignore what was said and pretend it never happened, while others say the first thing that comes to mind, no matter how unrelated it might be. If transitions or surprises are on the horizon, warn the student in advance. Have the student sit near others who are high in empathy and caring to increase the likelihood of positive interactions.

• *Give specific assignments.* Be very specific in what you want. For example, "John, please do numbers 1, 2, and 3. Come and tell me when you have finished." You might also arrange some other signal (a raised hand, head resting on the desk, etc.) if you are concerned about the student contacting you too frequently.

• *Provide schedules.* Give students a planner or visual schedule so they know what is happening throughout the day. If you teach in a block schedule, write the times of each part of the class on the board. For example:

7:20–7:40 Poetry
7:40–8 Reading
8–8:20 Writing
8:20–8:40 Questions/begin homework

Now a student who struggles in any one of these areas knows she only has to read for 20 minutes and the activity changes.

• *Grow interests through linking.* It is common for autistic students, in particular, to have an obsessive interest in some subject. To help grow more flexible thinking, try to link their obsessive interest to another subject being studied in class. For example, if a student is obsessed with Columbus as an explorer but the class is studying space travel, try to have the student connect Columbus's mode of exploration on the seas to space travel in the air.

• *Shorten or modify assignments.* Because excessive focus and distractibility can be problems, shorten or alter assignments. If too much material appears on a single page, many students won't know where to focus and will become confused.

• *Teach social skills and nuances.* Understanding and using the nuances of language and social interaction are often major issues for autistic students. Be sure to provide direct instruction when words have multiple meanings. Idioms, analogies, and sarcasm can easily be misunderstood, so explain such language carefully. Without pushing too hard, model, teach, and practice nonverbal communication skills such as tone of voice, body language, various facial expressions, and personal space. Provide visual cues to prompt social skills either informally or formally. Use visual scripts—situations presented on cards that ask the student to assess what's going on in certain social situations (Gagnon, 2001).

• *Use earphones to block sound.* When students appear unable to shut out extraneous sound, consider providing earphones.

Working with Difficult Parents

Although most parents are very supportive of teachers and feel good about their child's school and class, it has become more common for parents to blame teachers and administrators when problems arise. Rather than expecting their child to adapt, parents may attribute problems to the teacher's lack of sensitivity or poor instruction. A recent survey found that 31 percent of all teachers identified communicating with and involving parents as the biggest challenge they face (MetLife Survey, 2004). In light of the considerable stress parents can cause and the exacerbation of discipline problems when lacking their support, we offer some strategies here that can elicit increased cooperation among even the most difficult parents. (Some of what follows is borrowed or adapted from *Handling Difficult Parents* [Mendler, 2006]).

Strategies for Effective Interaction with Parents

The following strategies will help you build and sustain positive relationships with your students' parents.

• *View difficult parents as having something to learn.* Try to realize that an angry parent is better than an absent parent! Angry parents can be very unpleasant, but their anger conveys advocacy. As much as you might disagree with a parent's complaint, the fact that the parent is sharing it shows that she cares about her child. When we view complaints, anger, and threats as misguided advocacy, we're better able to continue working with the parent because the only issue becomes our disagreement with *what* is being advocated. Virtually all parents will cooperate if they really believe that you care about their child and are eager to help their child become successful.

• *View difficult parents as having something to teach.* If everybody cooperated, there would probably be little to learn. When pushed by difficult students or parents, educators have three options. They can try to avoid them, fight or argue back, or learn from them. Realistically, avoiding does not work. Parents know where to find us. Some will be omnipresent and very quick to complain about perceived wrongdoing. Fighting or arguing with them usually leads to more stress and conflict. As Henry Ford once said, "Failure is the opportunity to begin again a little more intelligently." Ask yourself what there might be to learn from a difficult parent. Try to allow yourself to get beyond your raw emotions and see things from the parent's perspective. What might be motivating this parent's anger?

Take Mrs. Skinner, for example. Mrs. Skinner's presence and complaints made teachers of Danny, her physically disabled and learning impaired son, roll their eyes upon seeing her. She was ornery, sarcastic, and caustic. She always seemed to focus

on the negative despite school professionals' many fine efforts
to accommodate her son. In actuality, her frustration was often
understandable as she struggled to get a supportive but rigid
school system to address her child's needs. She had an unyield-
ing devotion to Danny that pushed her to get needed services
for her son. Once school people understood that her abrasive
manner was merely a reflection of her dedication to her son, they
could better direct their energy toward brainstorming effective
learning strategies and needed services.

• *Be guided by what is educationally sound, not politically
correct.* Be guided by what you believe is in the best educational interests of your students. Teachers are on solid footing
when guided by two primary goals already cited in this book:
do everything in our power to help students be successful and
further the development of responsible student behavior. When
managing a tough situation, be guided by what is possible to
help your students be successful and what kinds of actions or
consequences are likely to teach them more about responsibility. Actions guided by these two goals will always be respected, if
not applauded. In addition, we need to reinforce the values most
parents want their children to learn. In some cases, we must
be prepared to teach the values that parents *should* want their
children to learn: responsibility, tolerance, safety, and the ability to effectively communicate with others. In this era, too many
educators are easily intimidated, believing that they will receive
little administrative support if parents complain. Focus on what
is educationally sound, while keeping an eye on what is politically correct. Although not all conflict between a teacher and
administrator generated by a complaining parent can be avoided,
much of it can.

• *Convey respect and dignity.* It's easy for well-mannered
people to act with respect and dignity when all is going well. The
challenge is to convey these attitudes when anger, disagreement,
and finger pointing are coming your way. In all interactions with
parents, respond to them in the same way you want them to

respond to you. Model what you expect. When you need to give feedback to a parent and are unsure what to say, try putting yourself at the receiving end of your message. If a parent gets mad and starts using language that you find offensive, act in a way that is consistent with what you're trying to teach your students. What would you want your students to say or do if they were being verbally assaulted? How would you want them to react? When your line has been crossed, set limits firmly yet respectfully.

• *Be quick to forgive and difficult to offend.* When working to get the best out of people, it's fine to hold them accountable for what they do, but be quick to forgive their transgressions. Don't clutter your "hard drive" with the spam of anger and resentment when others say or do hurtful things. Listen, respond, and be assertive when necessary, but be sure to hit your emotional delete button early and often when others say or do things that are irritating. Try to hear their concerns without being stung by the delivery.

• *Get on their side early.* Spend some time early in the school year figuring out who your challenging students are, and then make contact with their parents. Demonstrate interest by introducing yourself either in person or by phone. Tell them that you expect all of your students to be successful, and identify a few important guidelines that you expect your students to follow. Ask if they have any suggestions for things you can do to be a great teacher for their child. Quite simply, it is important to show that you care by enthusiastically expressing your desire to make it a successful year.

Caring goes a long way with parents and students. It is also important in other professions. Studying medical mistakes among doctors, Levinson and her colleagues (1997) found no difference in the medical mistakes between those who had been sued and those who had not. However, the research showed that physicians who had never been sued spent 20 percent more time with their patients and showed more personal interest than those who had. If physicians can avoid malpractice lawsuits by spending a few more caring minutes with a patient, it is reasonable to assume that teachers, too, can avoid a lot of bellyaching from parents by conveying the human touch.

• *Form a team.* Difficult students find it advantageous to keep parents and teachers battling each other. Many parents think their child does no wrong. Don't debate this view. Instead, emphasize how the child is hurting *himself* rather than how he is hurting you or the class. Invite parents to find things each of you can do to make the problem better. Parents are more willing to join with you to help their child than to help the school. Here are some examples of what you might say:

"He's falling behind in his work."

"She's getting in with a bad crowd."

"Your son really makes himself look immature when he behaves that way."

"He's letting himself down by doing less than his best."

"She's reducing her future options."

"He's becoming cynical about his future."

• *Ask, "What works at home?"* This question shows you respect what's happening at home. Many parents will tell. Others will tell you they don't know, in which case you might ask if they can brainstorm with you some things that they would recommend you try in the classroom.

• *Make at least two phone calls home before problems occur.* Your first phone call to a parent should be to introduce yourself and your program. Before school begins, tell parents that you are looking forward to having their child in your class this year. Be clear and specific in letting them know what factors are most important for success in your classroom (e.g., study skills, good organization). You might ask them to describe their child in terms of study habits and organizational skills. Ask them to tell you a little bit about their child's past school experience, how she best learns, and what interests she has. The second phone call should be made sometime during the first two weeks. Offer a genuine compliment about something the student accomplished either academically or behaviorally.

• *Send complimentary notes home occasionally.* Sending a note to parents about an achievement or accomplishment pertaining to their child often generates much support. Everyone likes to hear good news about their child.

• *Call and leave a positive message on voice mail.* To save time, simply call when you think nobody will be home and share a message of appreciation about something positive the student accomplished. Such a call can be especially useful after you have discussed a concern with a parent and notice improvement in the child. End with something like "Thanks for your help in influencing Krissy because improvement is definitely happening. If you want to call back, feel free, but there's really no need—I just wanted to let you know."

• *Solicit information from parents.* To be successful, let parents know that you would like help in understanding their child. Specifically, ask them these questions:

"What are three things your child likes to do?"

"What are a few things that your child has liked best about school?"

"What are two or three things you have noticed that help your child learn?"

"What are some things that I should know that could help me make school a successful place for your child?"

• *Ask to see pictures of the family.* This small gesture really has a big impact on how the parent will work with you. Most parents enjoy showing pictures of their children and appreciate your wanting to see them. Really look at the pictures and make a sincere comment or two about them.

• *Structure their lives with preplanned homework nights.* Say something like the following to your parents: "Mr. and Mrs. Ortega, I just want to let you know right now that there is one thing in this world I hate more than anything else: I hate when people waste my time. I don't feel like I have enough of it, and I can't stand when people waste it. So you're in luck, because this means I will always do my absolute best never to waste your time or your child's time. That means I will not be giving them homework every single night this year. On average, they will get homework two or three nights per week in this class, usually on Tuesdays and Thursdays. Moms and dads can now plan ahead on the nights their children have homework."

- *Explain that you will be fair to every student.* Add that this approach means you won't always be treating students in exactly the same way. Your goals are to help each student be successful and to learn more about responsibility. Be sure this point is clear to them. It is the most important concept for good parent relations.

- *Tell parents when they can contact you.* Many teachers feel stressed because they think they need to be on call 24/7 with parents. Tell parents specifically when you are available—for example, "I am available by e-mail from 3 to 4 on Tuesday and Thursday and by phone from 3 to 4 on Wednesday." Setting it up this way also allows you to look good if you answer at 6 p.m. on a Sunday. In other words, it's good practice to underpromise and overdeliver.

- *Tell parents you're always willing to listen to them about their son or daughter.* This also means you won't be talking to them about someone else's child. Parents sometimes complain about what you're doing for another student in the class. Do not tell them! Instead say, "Ms. Smith, I would never talk about your son or daughter to another parent, which means it would be very inappropriate for me to talk to you about another child. But I would be glad to talk to you about your son. What's the problem with his homework assignment?"

- *Be assertive.* Tell parents upfront that there will be times during the year they may not like or agree with a decision you make. Let them know you will always listen to them and consider their opinions and ideas. But sometimes after considering all of what they have to say, you will still do what you think is best for their child, even if they disagree. You might let them know that all they need to do is call and say, "I disagree because . . . ."

Tips for Responding to Inappropriate Behavior from Parents

Despite your best efforts at fostering effective relationships with parents, they still may behave in inappropriate ways. Here are some strategies for addressing such flare-ups.

* *Allow the parent to let off some steam, but with limits.* Then try to diffuse the parent. Say something like "I know you're angry, Mrs. Jones, but swearing at me won't solve this problem."
* *Move around to refocus your nervous energy.* Moving will help you expel energy that might otherwise make you say something you'll regret.
* *Become softer, quieter, and slower.* If a parent turns up his volume, simply turn down yours.
* *Acknowledge the legitimacy of the complaint.* For example, you might say, "You're saying that your son thinks I'm unfair and boring. To better understand, what can you tell me about him that might help me get his interest and best effort?"
* *Call the parent before you send his child to the office.* The phone call can sound something like this: "Mr. Shaw, Andy has been having some trouble using proper language these last few days, and when I correct him, he has been getting angry with me. Before I get him involved with the office, I wanted to request your assistance. I wonder if you have any ideas about how to help him."
* *Separate the student and his parent.* If the student is present when the parent attacks inappropriately, ask the child to step out of the room for a moment, and then address the parent. Say something like "Ms. Richards, I know you're upset, but I don't want Jose to get the idea that it's OK to talk to adults in that tone of voice. Please do not talk to me like that." Immediately take charge by redirecting the conversation back on task. Later on, when all seems calm, you might invite the student back into the room.

• *Simply say, "Please don't talk to me like that."* Setting a boundary for appropriate interaction like this may be enough to defuse the situation.

• *Focus on the future.* Shift your and the parent's perspective away from the heat of the moment by saying something like "Mrs. Lewis, what do you think we can do to help Steve avoid this kind of situation in the future?" or "Maybe you can visit with Steve tonight so he understands there are better choices he can make. Thanks for your support."

• *Be the good guy.* Let the parent know the consequence could have been worse. Say something like "Ms. Hill, usually cheating means a 0 and a detention. But I'm going to go to bat for Tony. Since this is his first time, I think the 0 is sufficient, and I'll advise the principal against the detention. I can't promise she'll see it this way, but I'll do my best."

• *Explain the difference between "fair" and "equal" treatment.* When parents complain about unfair treatment toward their child, you can say many things, but our favorite is "I know the consequence I gave Joe [the other student]. But we're not here to talk about him. What's the problem with the consequence *your* child got?"

Discipline in Urban Schools

We have seen positive initiatives to improve achievement and behavior in urban schools. Many of these initiatives are making a difference. Just recently, for example, one of the authors visited an inner-city elementary school that begins each day with a Boys Group for students with very high suspension rates. The group gives these students the opportunity to talk about issues, set daily goals, and learn effective nonviolent problem-solving skills. Since the program's start six months earlier, only one student has been suspended once, and many students have gone on to become peer mediators.

Unfortunately, most urban schools continue to struggle

with serious issues, including a hardening of both teachers and students, decaying infrastructure, and scarce resources. One school we visited had a problem because many of the 3rd and 4th grade students had their sneakers stolen off their feet on the way to school. Too often, children need to walk the same streets to school that rang out with gunshots the night before. Is it any wonder that many children might feel preoccupied with challenges other than academics?

In Rochester, New York, home to two of the authors of this book, 51 percent of urban families are female-headed with kids living in poverty. Overall, 36 percent of families with children are living in poverty in cities compared with 7 percent in the suburbs (according to U.S. Census Bureau statistics for 2006). Although poverty can be found in all settings, we choose to emphasize specific ideas and suggestions for urban educators due to the ever-increasing concentration of people living in large cities.

With the rapid rise in the United States' immigrant population, the face of American cities is rapidly changing. Some urban schools with English as a Second Language programs have students representing as many as 150 different languages in the community. Large numbers of people from diverse cultures continue to compete for sparse low-income housing, jobs, and other resources. Under conditions where there simply isn't enough to go around, tensions among groups naturally increase. City schools usually reflect the same tensions as the city itself. Each cultural group has its own standards and rites of passage. Different actions challenge pride and dignity for each group.

At its best, the richness of each culture brings energy and excitement that provide opportunities for students to learn through experience about others—their customs, values, and historic contributions. Cities offer a variety of resources that cannot be matched in the suburbs. The arts, business and industry, parks, museums, and a multitude of people are all within reach for the creative inner-city teacher. For every turned-off "street student," there are dozens of eager youngsters who want to

learn. We were touched by an 8th grade class in a human relations course at an overcrowded school in a poor neighborhood
in the Bronx. One student shared that her family had their extra
money hidden under the living room rug. A classmate asked why
this girl would reveal such confidential information. She replied,
"In this class you are all my friends; I trust you." The sigh from all
her classmates indicated the closeness of the moment.

It is exciting to hear about, observe, and in some cases work
with schools that do a great job fostering resilience in its students and getting excellent results in very challenging places. We
have already described much of what these schools and teachers do throughout this book. In this section, we highlight strategies that may sound familiar but are particularly important with
students who too often have to face life issues that can interrupt
and disrupt their learning.

Keys to Success for Urban Educators

The following keys to success involve creating and sustaining
classrooms and schools where students feel *connected*, *competent*, and in *control*.

• *Ask yourself three important questions to emphasize
prevention:*

What can I do as a teacher to help all my students feel connected to each other and to me?

What can I do to emphasize achievement while making it
really hard for my students to fail?

What can I do that encourages all of my students to know
that their voice matters, they can make a difference, and
their opinion counts?

• *Believe success is achievable.* Virtually every recommen-
dation for improving education includes having "high expectations." Sadly, this is increasingly coming to mean that curriculum
at a "high" level will be taught, not necessarily learned. In a large

urban school district in the Midwest where we have been invited to do extensive consulting and training, *pacing* is the current buzzword used to describe how every teacher needs to cover the same material for all students within a specific time frame. Many of these well-meaning but very stressed teachers say that the material is beyond the instructional level of up to two-thirds of their classes! They are essentially asking several students to perform at a frustration level without realizing that the motivation and discipline problems they need help with are in large part directly caused by this teaching approach.

The goal for every student in every class should be to "Get better today than you were yesterday in whatever needs to be learned." Throughout this book, we have espoused the importance of encouraging students to be competitive with themselves rather than each other. For example, ask, "If you can write one line today, can you do two tomorrow?" "What did *you* get better at this period, day, week, month, and year?" ought to be the mantra in every class to every student. Schools and their students ought to be recognized for progress even if that progress doesn't always bring a student up to "grade level."

A major research project analyzing elementary school achievement over the last 15 years in Chicago identified 144 public elementary inner-city schools that had shown substantial and sustained improvement in reading test scores through grade 8 (Designs for Change, 2005). The typical school's performance reached national averages. The "Five Essential Supports for Student Learning" that were consistently found in successful schools were Effective School Leadership, Social Supports for Student Learning, Family and Community Partnerships, Adult Collaboration and Development, and Quality Learning Activities. A safe atmosphere conducive to learning and the engagement of all learners in "challenging educational activities" was particularly noted. We believe a challenging educational activity is one that requires a reachable stretch for each student. It's fine to have a finish line, but there needs to be both recognition and appreciation that although all can finish, not all can or will finish first.

• *Know your students, and let your students know you.* Students learn best when they trust their teacher and are comfortable in their surroundings. Using open communication, establish an atmo-sphere of information sharing to build trust in your classroom. See it as your professional responsibility to make positive, con-sistent connections with your students. Know how your students naturally communicate. Make sure that you aren't offended by language that may be natural for your students but may sound rough or uncouth to you. Learn their likes and dislikes. Find out what classroom privileges are meaningful to them and which are perceived as hokey or viewed as undesirable chores.

In addition, it is equally important for your students to know you. Some teachers erroneously think they must keep their guard up at all times. Although it is a good idea to be on guard in a potentially hostile environment, doing so with your students will guarantee that your classroom will have walls between you and them.

• *Provide a supportive relationship.* Wang, Haertel, & Walberg (1997), among others, note that a teacher's concern, high expec-tations, and role modeling are key protective factors that miti-gate against the likelihood of academic failure, particularly for students in difficult life circumstances. We have long advocated for a Big Brothers Big Sisters–type program right in school where caring adults "adopt" one or two students (not currently in one's class) and provide mentoring and guidance on a regular basis.

• *Respect social and cultural differences, but teach behaviors needed for success at school.* Many kids from the street live by a set of norms to help them survive that are simultaneously harmful to their success at school. For example, physical fight-ing may be necessary to survive on the street, but it will always lead to major consequences at school. Students need to hear that our voices are consistent with their reality. When working to teach them alternatives, we must start by acknowledging their strengths. Many of the self-control strategies offered in Chapter 8 can be particularly helpful. Even if a student seems to have little or no interest in doing something different, perhaps we can succeed in getting him to wait until he is out of school that day and has a chance to cool off.

• *Provide appropriate outlets for expressing feelings for students and the teacher.* Some urban students put on a "front," meaning they try to appear cool and detached, as if nothing bothers them. In their mind, this approach is considered a sign of maturity and strength. But the reality is that they have feelings just like anyone else. As the Beatles say in "Hey Jude," "Being cool only makes the world a little colder." And because these feelings are often hidden under the guise of being cool, they can and do intensify. Learn the language of "coolness," and provide acceptable outlets for feelings to be expressed. Make sharing a regular but optional part of each day. The use of anonymous techniques, like a gripe box or suggestion box, is especially useful.

• *Welcome parents at school.* Students with at least one parent who is strongly aware of what is going on at school and who communicates the value of education are far more likely to succeed than students who don't. Adult education programs offered at school in which parents can work toward a GED or equivalent will begin getting parents to value education while their children are going to school. We believe in a novel idea: Schools should open their doors to all adults who did not graduate from high school and offer them opportunities to take classes. Make the signs at school welcoming, too. For example, "We Are Glad You Are Visiting Our School" should precede "We Do Ask That All Visitors Sign In at the Office upon Entering." A dedicated "parent" room that has coffee, donuts, and books on parenting and scheduled seminars on how to help children learn at home are two other strategies that are often well received.

• *Provide help during and after school for students who need it.* Have tutors available to assist with assignments. Also, be sure students know they are welcome to stay after school to do their homework or get assistance. Students lacking effort who are failing should be required to stay after school for help until they get up to speed.

• *Make school the hub of community activity.* School is the one place in many urban areas where all neighborhood students gather. We believe it is therefore in a unique position to be the primary source from which people in the community receive the services they need. For example, it may be a lot easier to coordinate parent conferences at school if families' government assistance checks were awaiting them in an office inside the school after the conference. At the same time, if adult education classes were offered right after school with babysitting or after-school activities simultaneously provided for children, it is likely more adults would attend. Too often in needy communities, many agencies and initiatives operate independently and lack coordination. Schools also should be the center of after-school activities offered for students so they have a safe place to do their homework or participate in recreational activities.

• *Enlist community leaders.* Contact as many community leaders as possible and ask to meet with them on a regular basis. Every city has both formal and informal groups that help the community. Some examples might be the local YMCA, the NAACP, a church group, or a cultural center. Find out what their programs offer, what support they can give, and what support you can give them. Invite them into your class to talk with students. Be sure to ask for any cultural insights that could be affecting student performance in the classroom so you can better understand subtle changes that might make a difference.

• *Give students practice in leading, making decisions, and giving input.* A major thrust of our approach with all students is teaching responsibility. We have sometimes heard inner-city teachers tell us that the only thing that works is to yell at or threaten "these kids" because that is what they get at home. Although we are not privy to being inside everybody's home, it is clear that students who lack opportunities to think, decide, and make choices in their home need more practice with these behaviors at school. The only way to learn responsibility is to have opportunities to practice the subset of skills: planning, predicting, and decision making.

• *Capitalize on the resources in the city.* Working independently or with a group of other teachers, use the city itself as a teaching laboratory for experiences related to your content. Visit businesses, hospitals, the police station, museums, libraries, planetariums, historical landmarks, and other spots that are sometimes taken for granted. Arrange trips to the nearest rural areas whenever possible. Some city children never see a live cow until they are adults. Bring city resources into your school if you cannot take students out. One school made an arrangement with a local college to let its architectural students transform a hallway into an arboretum and another hallway into a library, and to build time-out areas in five classrooms.

• *Focus on the positive.* As emphasized by the developers of the FISH philosophy, in which businesses apply lessons to maximize satisfaction in workers and customers (Lundin, Christensen, & Paul, 2002), it is so important to choose your attitude and brighten your students' day. Kids need upbeat, respectful teachers who build on the positive. Limit your corrections on writing assignments to one or two manageable improvements. Once the student has mastered those skills, find one or two more things to work on. Focus on the positive with your fellow teachers as well. Look for ways to make the school a better, safer place. It is better to suggest an improvement than it is to comment on what is wrong. By increasing the positive energy of the faculty and, most important, of yourself, you will reduce your own stress related to working in the inner city and help make the school a better place for you and your students.

• *Develop group support with other teachers.* Share your feelings openly. Teaching is traditionally done alone, with the teacher isolated from the rest of the faculty except for informal discussions in faculty lounges or lunchrooms. Because of the intensity of trying to reach many challenging students, isolation and frustration can result. As we stated earlier, one of the most important reasons for the success of our in-service training programs is the process of teachers sharing with other teachers how they feel, what their problems are, and what can be done to make the school a better place.

• *Constantly share realistic alternatives.* Urban students from impoverished areas often tell us they want to be professional football or basketball players. Many others want to be the next great rapper. Although teachers should never attempt to kill a student's dreams, it is our responsibility to point out viable alternatives should the lofty original goal not be met. For example, if by 11th grade a student has not yet made the varsity team, the probability of making the NBA is extraordinary. Great teachers point out other occupations associated with basketball, explaining that a student might not make it to the NBA but could become a physical education teacher and be around sports all the time. Students could also aspire to coach or referee, making a nice living being around the sport they love. Students who desperately want to be rap stars can be shown that working in music production studios might be an option, too.

• *Remember the Bottom Line.* To conclude this chapter, we offer an anonymous poem that you can copy, blow up, and post in your classrooms.

The Bottom Line

Face it.
Nobody owes you a living.
What you achieve or fail to achieve in your lifetime
is directly related to what you do
or fail to do.
No one chooses his parents or childhood
but you can choose your own direction.
Everyone has problems and obstacles to overcome
but that too is relative to each individual.

Nothing is carved in stone.
You can change anything in your life
if you want to badly enough.
Excuses are for losers.
Those who take responsibility for their actions
are the real winners in life.
Winners meet life's challenges head on
knowing there are no guarantees
and give it all they've got.
It's never too late or too early to begin.
Time plays no favorites
and will pass whether you act or not.

Take control of your life.
Dare to dream and take risks.
If you aren't willing to work for your goals,
don't expect others to.

Believe in yourself!

—Anonymous

❧ Conclusion ❧

When one of the authors first listened to the Rolling Stones, his mother said, "That's not music—that's noise." He replied, "I bet that's what your mother said to you about Frank Sinatra." She said, "I think you're right. She just might have said that." He said, "I'm never saying that to my children." Then he heard them playing Nine Inch Nails, and without thinking, he said, "That's not music—that's noise!"

It is not our job to tell children how bad their world is, especially by comparing it with ours. Although to many of us theirs seems worse than ours in many ways, our job is to help them thrive and navigate the world in which they live. We played outside; they Web chat. We dated and had dances; they have Facebook and MySpace. We played sports; they have Gameboys. Every generation is different, but they all have in common growing up in a fearful world, full of uncertainty, danger, and seemingly unsolvable problems. From World War I, the Great Depression, World War II and the Holocaust, the Cold War (remember practicing duck and cover?) to terrorism, no one escapes the surrounding world.

All of us, regardless of our generation, grapple with our world, our society, our families, our friends, and ourselves. We believe that school can give children the gift of making sense of it all and receiving the necessary tools to allow them not only to rise above it but to make things better for others.

Teachers frequently ask us, "What difference can I make? I only have them [pick a time: for an hour, a day, once a week, 15 minutes]. They come from homes with [pick a condition: physical abuse, alcohol or drug abuse, emotional abuse, poverty]."

We are resolute in our answer. One hour is better than none. Fifteen minutes is better than none. Your time with this child might be the only time during the day when he feels secure, welcome, productive, and important. Every minute feeling this is one less minute feeling something else. All children, no matter how they behave, deserve to feel safe, secure, and cared about, even if for only a few minutes every day.

Many children come to school because it's safer than home. Others test us with intolerable behavior to see if we will stand by them when the going gets rough. Still others do not believe in themselves and do not care what happens to them. So, yes, an hour or 15 minutes is better than nothing.

We hope this book helps all who read it to become more understanding and skilled in handling all children, but especially those who make themselves unlikable and irritating. They weren't born angry and unmotivated. We really hope this book helps you help these kids find a way to make their lives any kind of music they choose. Thanks.

Appendix A

❧ Practice Scenarios ❧

Below are 8 real-life situations that teachers asked us to help them handle within the past year. The situations are given on the first page without our response. We encourage you to put yourself in the shoes of the teacher. Then pretend you are a consultant. How would you advise a colleague to handle the situation? The situations are great for faculty meeting discussion and role-playing. Following the listing of eight situations, we revisit each in turn and provide our response.

Situation 1: Your school has a policy that says, "No jackets or sweatshirts in class." Jennifer is wearing a sweatshirt again. You ask her to take it off. She refuses. You then tell her to stay after class to discuss the rule and she says, "I ain't coming late because you know this is a stupid rule!" The class is waiting for your response. What do you say?

Situation 2: You give the class a homework assignment and Chris asks out loud, "Why do we have to do this?" He then says that doing 12 problems is ridiculous and he's not going to do them all. The class looks at you. How do you respond to Chris and the class?

Situation 3: You begin to start your lesson but your students are continuing to talk to each other. You tell them to stop but they ignore you and continue talking anyway. How do you get them to stop talking?

Situation 4: You have a class of 26 students. You begin teaching and notice Russell has his head down. Upon closer inspection you notice a swollen right eye. You are positive it was not there yesterday. How do you handle the situation?

Situation 5: Your policy says, "Late work is minus 5 points per day." Kiara's summer reading assignment was due right after summer break. On December 9, not aware of the policy, she hands you her paper. Do you take it? And if so, how do you grade it?

Situation 6: Melanie is in your 5th grade class and has been working on her behavior all week. It is obvious she has made tremendous progress. You say to the class, "Melanie has been working really hard on her behavior this week and I am really proud of her. Because she has been so good she gets an extra 15 minutes on the playground!" What major mistake are you making by giving her the extra 15 minutes?

Situation 7: You teach an inclusion social studies class. On the unit test Paul gets 30 minutes of extended time and Amy gets no extended time. They are best friends. Amy's mom calls and complains that it is not fair because her daughter got less time than Paul. What do you say to Amy's mom?

Situation 8: You are at a staff development day and call back to school to see how things are going. You find out that the class is completely out of control. You are aware that when you are out of the building they almost never behave for the sub. What could you have done before you left to get your class to behave when you were gone?

Here are the situations again. But this time below each situation is our response.

Situation 1: Your school has a policy that says, "No jackets or sweatshirts in class." Jennifer is wearing a sweatshirt again. You ask her to take it off. She refuses. You then tell her to stay after class to discuss the rule and she says, "I ain't staying because you know this is a stupid rule!" The class is waiting for your response. What do you say?

Our response: Don't argue or get trapped into a power struggle. Instead, say something like, "Much as I wish I had some say about that rule, unfortunately I don't. It is a school rule and if you want to try to get it changed, I'll set you up with (Principal, School Board) and if you can convince them to change it, I won't ever hassle you again. But until then, thanks for taking it off." If the student continues to refuse, ignore and deal with him later. If he or another student challenges you on his "insubordination," remind your class that you do not always stop instruction to handle an incident of misbehavior and assure them that you and the student will deal with this later. Some administrators ask us if we are undermining them by giving this response. We don't think so. Teachers do not have to agree with every rule. However, they should enforce every rule. Wouldn't it be great if a police officer responded like this when giving you a speeding ticket.

Officer: Here's your ticket for speeding.
Speeder: But that speed limit is ridiculous. It should be 65 not 40.
Officer: I totally agree. And if I was in charge I would probably change it. But I'm not, so here's your ticket. Sorry.

Situation 2: You give the class a homework assignment and Chris asks out loud, "Why do we have to do this?" He then says that doing 12 problems is ridiculous and he's not going to do them all. The class looks at you. How do you respond to Chris and the class?

Our response: With kids like Chris it is almost always best to address them after class. However, since he took you on in front of the group you might respond right then in the following way:

Teacher: So you don't want to do 12 problems. How many do you feel you should have to do?
Chris: None.
Teacher: Well none is not an option, but I can live with 7. In fact (looking at the entire class), why don't you each pick any 7 that are going to best show me you understand the material. Or better yet, do the 7 easiest on the page. And Chris, great job getting these guys 5 less problems. You all might want to thank him later!

The teacher has now made Chris look good in front of his friends. It is now much easier to pull Chris aside as everyone is leaving. Then the conversation goes like this:

Teacher: Chris, when you want something from me yelling it out in front of everyone probably is not the best approach. Do you think you can come up with a more appropriate way to talk to me next time?
Chris: I guess I can talk to you privately, and not yell out in class.
Teacher: Great. And good job Chris. I'm sure everyone is really happy with you.

A key is to assign more work than you really want students to do. If you want the kids to do 10 problems assign them 15. This way when they argue you can negotiate down, make yourself look really good, and still get exactly what you wanted in the first place!

Situation 3: You begin to start your lesson but your students are continuing to talk to each other. You tell them to stop but they ignore you and continue talking anyway. How do you get them to stop talking?

Our response: Stop trying to get them to stop talking!!

We like to say that if you are a great reader in school you spend your entire life on honor roll. If you are a great talker in school you spend your entire life in detention. OK, maybe we're exaggerating. Great public speakers, the kids that are going to be comedians or actors often spend their lives in trouble. Instead of telling them to stop talking try this:

Teacher: It seems like there is non-stop talking going on here. I don't want to take that away from you. So I've decided to give you 3 minutes to talk to each other (pick what works for you, but remember, always start with a number you are willing to negotiate from. In this example the teacher is really OK with 6 minutes, but is starting with 3.) Would you prefer 3 minutes at the beginning, middle or end of class?
Student: 3 minutes?! That's nothing!
Teacher: Well what do you think would be a fair number?
Students: 10 minutes.
Teacher: 10 is too many. But I can live with 5. How does that sound?
Students: 7 minutes.
Teacher: Let's agree on 6. But I trust that after 6 minutes the talking will stop and I won't have to argue with any of you, correct?

There is still a chance that the students will continue talking after 6 minutes. But if it continues now you can say to your class, "You're the ones who told me you would stop after 6 minutes. Are you all saying you don't know how to make decisions for yourselves? That's upsetting. I guess I can start making all the decisions around here from now on!"

Situation 4: You have a class of 26 students. You begin teaching and notice Russell has his head down. Upon closer inspection you notice a swollen right eye. You are positive it was not there yesterday. How do you handle the situation?

Our response: Try your best to get the class started on some sort of group activity that frees you up to wander the room. Then approach Russell and use a strategy we call the two-minute intervention. Get close to Russell and begin asking him questions not related to the eye. If he doesn't respond at all, then answer the question yourself. For example:

Teacher: Russell, what's up? You look tired. Are you tired?
Russell: No response.
Teacher: Because sometimes I'm tired when I'm here and I get paid to be here. So I would totally understand if you were. If I could do one thing to make this class better for you what would it be?

The goal with this dialogue is to get Russell comfortable with talking to you. After this relationship is built you can ask him what happened to his eye. The relationship needs to come first or you can almost guarantee he will shrug or tell you he doesn't want to talk about it. This is a time to bring in a counselor, social worker, psychologist, or administrator, especially if you suspect some type of abuse going on at the home.

Situation 5: Kiara's summer reading assignment was due right after summer break. A few days after school has begun, she hands you her paper. Do you take it? Do you deduct from her grade?

Our response: We believe it is educationally unsound to not accept an assignment. After all, isn't our entire purpose to take what students do and make them better at whatever it is they did? Try not to get locked into predetermining consequences for make-up or late work. Instead, say something like this to your class:

Teacher: I always encourage you to do make-up work in this class. I encourage you to make up a test or quiz if you get a low grade. Also, it is never too late to hand in an assignment.
Student: Well what grade will we get if we hand in a paper really late?
Teacher: I don't know. You see, your grade on any make-up work will take a whole bunch of factors into consideration. I will look at how hard you worked the first time. How hard you worked the second time. I will look at how good your attitude was the first time and how good your attitude was the second time. And then after the make-up work is complete, you and I together will determine a grade that you think you deserve. Sound good??

It's the same with late work. Tell them that after the work is handed in you and the students will have a conversation about why it was so late and what grade they feel they deserve. Now it is always in everyone's interest to do the work. And learning should always be most important.

Situation 6: Melanie is in your 5th grade class and has been working on her behavior all week. It is obvious she has made tremendous progress. You say to the class, "Melanie has been working really hard on her behavior this week and I am really proud of her. Because she has been so good she gets an extra 15 minutes on the playground!" What major mistake are you making by giving her the extra 15 minutes?

Our response: Many teachers believe that if they reward Melanie other students will want to be more like her. But instead, many are thinking, "Whatever. With stupid Melanie, I don't care."

Or, "I'm always good and I didn't get anything." When we reward one person, or a small group of people, but we leave others out, we almost always create the animosity that can lead to bullying. So instead, try this:

Teacher: I just want to tell you that I am really proud of Melanie. She has behaved herself really well this week and because Melanie has been so good this week you all get an extra 15 minutes on the playground in honor of her. Do not even consider thanking me!! I had nothing to do with it. And if I were the rest of you, I'd thank Melanie. Have fun.

Rewards are most effective when everybody gains in honor of the specific student. Instead of being annoyed with Melanie the class is congratulating her. Positive peer pressure often occurs. Some students might even think, "Melanie, if you need help being good again next week, let me know!"

Situation 7: You teach an inclusion social studies class. On the unit test Paul gets 30 minutes of extended time and Amy gets no extended time. They are best friends. Amy's mom calls and complains that it is not fair because her daughter got less time than Paul. What do you say to Amy's mom?

Our response: It is important to tell parents early in the year that you will always do your best to be fair to each of their children which means you will not always be treating them exactly the same way. The whole concept of inclusion is that different students get different assignments, tests, quizzes, etc. As a teacher it is important that we tell parents we will always talk to them about their child, but we will not discuss other children with them. With that being said, the conversation goes like this.

Teacher: Mrs. Amy, I understand you are upset. Are you saying your daughter needs more time?

Mrs. Amy: Well Paul gets…

Teacher: I know what Paul gets, but just like I would never talk about Amy to another parent, I cannot talk about other children to you. I'm sure you understand. But I will always talk to you about Amy. Do you think she needs more time? She didn't ask for it.

Mrs. Amy: Yes. She wasn't finished.

Teacher: Oh I'm sorry. In the future if she isn't finished she can just raise her hand and let me know. Sound good?

As soon as the teacher tries justifying what she's doing for Paul she's in big trouble. Try hard to turn the conversation back to their child. Avoid the trap of feeling compelled to treat all students the same way.

Situation 8: You are at a staff development day and call back to school to see how things are going. You find out that the class is completely out of control. You are aware that when you are out of the building they almost never behave for the sub. What could you have done before you left to get your class to behave when you were gone?

Our response: This is the perfect time to challenge your students and address the need for control. Many teachers try to threaten. But challenge is much more effective.

Pull the leader(s) aside (usually your most problematic students when you are not around) and tell them something like this:

"I am going to be out of school tomorrow and I look forward to hearing great things from the sub about how the class behaved. You guys are really in charge tomorrow. In fact, if it was up to me, I'd give each of you the sub pay! I know you can get the class to mess around when I'm gone but I'm not so sure you can get everyone to behave. I guess we'll see when I get back." You might conclude with letting them know you will be calling them after school to hear how things went.

By empowering the leaders you make them feel strong and important. By challenging you make them want to prove you wrong. And in order to do so they have to get everyone else in class to behave.

❧ School Discipline Survey ❧

Directions

1. Each participant responds to Scales 1–9 (pp. 232–240).
2. Each participant fills in the "Individual Data Summary" (p. 241).
3. The group leader collects the summary sheets and fills in the Team Data Summary (p. 242).

Examine the results. See areas of agreement and disagreement. Discuss, interpret, and use for future faculty development activities.

Note: These instruments may be used by teachers or schools without permission but may not be reproduced for distribution or included in any publication without written permission of the publisher.

Scale 1. Goal Clarity and Conflict
Things About Discipline Procedures

Read each statement and then circle the lettered response that best represents the situation in your school.

Statement I—I often wonder what is the basic procedure for school discipline here. There are people in the school (maybe even myself) who spend a lot of time and energy doing things that are not consistent with what I think our main objectives for discipline ought to be. They downplay or overlook important parts of our total objective, or their time is directed at things I think aren't very important.

Statement II—The school's basic overall objectives regarding discipline procedures are very clear to me. All of my and everyone else's efforts seem directly related to accomplishing these key goals. Whenever a question arises over what things need to be done, we are able to set priorities by referring to our basic objectives.

 a. Statement I
 b. More Statement I than II
 c. Between Statement I and II
 d. More Statement II than I
 e. Statement II

Example(s): In the space below, describe one or more examples of situations in the school that illustrate your response on Scale 1.

_____

_____

_____

_____

Scale 2. Role Ambiguity
Things About How My Job Is Affected by Discipline

Statement I—Often situations arise on the job when I'm not certain what I am supposed to do. Frequently, I'm not even sure if a discipline situation is my responsibility or someone else's. We never get together to discuss what each individual thinks he (she) and the others on the job can or should do to work together to do the best job.

Statement II—In almost every discipline situation I am very sure about what responsibilities I have and about what others in the school are supposed to be doing. These discipline responsibilities are often discussed by relevant members of the school, particularly when someone has a question about what he or someone else should be doing.

    a. Statement I
    b. More Statement I than II
    c. Between Statement I and II
    d. More Statement II than I
    e. Statement II

Example(s):

_____

_____

_____

_____

Scale 3. Role Conflict
Clarity of Expectations

Statement I—Different people on the job expect different things from me in regard to working with students who misbehave. Often these get in the way of each other, or there just isn't enough time to meet everyone's demand. My job makes me feel like a juggler with too many balls.

Statement II—I have no trouble in doing the different things that the job and other people in school expect of me. I understand why I'm supposed to do things I do, and it all seems to fit together. If I feel as though the demands people in the school make of me are getting too heavy or don't make sense, we resolve the problem with a discussion.

    a. Statement I

    b. More Statement I than II

    c. Between Statement I and II

    d. More Statement II than I

    e. Statement II

Example(s):

_____

_____

_____

_____

Scale 4. Participation/Influence
How Staff Is Involved in Decision Making

Statement I—When some people try to participate in a discussion of discipline methods, they often get cut off, or their suggestions seem to die. People only seem to pay attention to some people and not others. Some people seem to do most of the talking while others don't participate very much.

Statement II—All participants get a chance to express themselves and to influence the group in discussions about discipline. We listen to every person's contributions and try to discuss the strong points in each. No one is ignored. Everyone is drawn into the discussion.

    a. Statement I
    b. More Statement I than II
    c. Between Statement I and II
    d. More Statement II than I
    e. Statement II

Example(s):

_____

_____

_____

_____

Scale 5. Commitment/Understanding
How Discipline Decisions Get Made Around Here

Directions: This scale is different from the previous ones. In this scale, read all the statements and circle the letter next to the one statement that most closely describes the general situation in your team.

When a disagreement arises among the faculty about a school-wide discipline issue:

   a. We assume it's probably best not to let it get personal, so we let it pass hoping it will cool down and eventually be forgotten. If it does start to ruffle feelings, we try to smooth the feelings and make the least of the disagreement (e.g., "Well, there is really no point in fighting about it, so let's forget it" or "We're all grownups; we shouldn't argue").

   b. Often we end the disagreement when someone takes charge and makes a decision or decides not to discuss it any further.

   c. We try to come to an agreement somewhere between the two disagreeing positions. In other words, we compromise. That way everyone gets a little and everyone gives a little, and the disagreement is taken care of.

   d. We get the disagreeing parties together and have them talk to each other about their points of view until each party can see some logic in the other's ideas. Then we try to come to an agreement that makes sense to everyone.

Example(s):

_____

_____

_____

_____

Scale 6. Conflict Management
How Discipline Affects What It's Like to Work Around Here

Statement I—I often get the feeling that some people in the school don't think that some other people in the school have much of a contribution to make. Some faculty don't pay much attention to the problems or suggestions of others. People are often taken for granted, and many prefer to neither see nor hear discipline problems.

Statement II—Everyone recognizes that the job could not be done without the cooperation and contribution of everyone else. Each person, including myself, is treated as an important part of the school team. When you bring up an idea or a problem, people sit up and take notice. It makes you feel that you and your job are important. People are receptive to unpleasant feelings associated with discipline problems and are eager to help each other.

    a. Statement I
    b. More Statement I than II
    c. Between Statement I and II
    d. More Statement II than I
    e. Statemcnt II

Example(s):

_____

_____

_____

_____

Scale 7. Recognition/Involvement
Style of Discipline

Statement I—My style of discipline really gets me down. People do not seem concerned with helping each other get the job done. Everyone is pulling in opposite directions; everyone is out for him- or herself. If you try to do something different, you get jumped on by people for being out of line; or if you make a mistake, you never hear the end of it.

Statement II—I really like my style of discipline, and I like working in this school. The team encourages you to take responsibility. You feel really appreciated by other staff members when you do a good job. When things aren't going well, people really make an effort to help each other. We really pull together on this team.

    a. Statement I

    b. More Statement I than II

    c. Between Statement I and II

    d. More Statement II and I

    e. Statement II

Example(s):

_____

_____

_____

_____

Scale 8. Support/Cohesiveness
Clarity of Consequences

Statement I—When students break school rules, they can never be sure of what will happen to them. The absence of consistently applied consequences for student misbehavior creates a chaotic school climate.

Statement II—Consequences of misbehavior are clearly understood by all students. When rules are broken, students know exactly what will happen to them. The school's discipline policy creates an orderly, organized school climate.

    a. Statement I
    b. More Statement I than II
    c. Between Statement I and II
    d. More Statement II than I
    e. Statement II

Example(s):

_____

_____

_____

_____

Scale 9. Consistency/Inconsistency
What the Methods of Discipline Are Around Here

Statement I—I often get locked into power struggles with unruly students. I find myself saying and doing things that I know are ineffective or inappropriate, but I just haven't found any more effective alternatives.

Statement II—Discipline isn't really a problem for me, because my style and methods are usually effective in preventing and stopping student misbehavior. I believe that at least some of my methods could help other teachers that have greater problems in working with unruly students.

    a. Statement I
    b. More Statement I than II
    c. Between Statement I and II
    d. More Statement II than I
    e. Statement II

Example(s):

_____

_____

_____

_____

Individual Data Summary
Scales

1. Goal Clarity and Conflict   I $\overline{\quad_a \qquad b \qquad c \qquad d \qquad_e}$ II

2. Role Ambiguity   I $\overline{\quad_a \qquad b \qquad c \qquad d \qquad_e}$ II

3. Role Conflict   I $\overline{\quad_a \qquad b \qquad c \qquad d \qquad_e}$ II

4. Participation/Influence   I $\overline{\quad_a \qquad b \qquad c \qquad d \qquad_e}$ II

5. Commitment/Understanding   I $\overline{\quad_a \qquad b \qquad c \qquad d \qquad_e}$ II

6. Conflict Management   I $\overline{\quad_a \qquad b \qquad c \qquad d \qquad_e}$ II

7. Recognition/Involvement   I $\overline{\quad_a \qquad b \qquad c \qquad d \qquad_e}$ II

8. Support/Cohesiveness   I $\overline{\quad_a \qquad b \qquad c \qquad d \qquad_e}$ II

9. Consistency/Inconsistency   I $\overline{\quad_a \qquad b \qquad c \qquad d \qquad_e}$ II

Team Data Summary
Scales

1. Goal Clarity and Conflict   I —— a —— b —— c —— d —— e —— II

2. Role Ambiguity   I —— a —— b —— c —— d —— e —— II

3. Role Conflict   I —— a —— b —— c —— d —— e —— II

4. Participation/Influence   I —— a —— b —— c —— d —— e —— II

5. Commitment/Understanding   I —— a —— b —— c —— d —— e —— II

6. Conflict Management   I —— a —— b —— c —— d —— e —— II

7. Recognition/Involvement   I —— a —— b —— c —— d —— e —— II

8. Support/Cohesiveness   I —— a —— b —— c —— d —— e —— II

9. Consistency/Inconsistency   I —— a —— b —— c —— d —— e —— II

❧ Bibliography ❧

Antoniou, A. S., Polychroni, P., & Vlachakis, A. N. (2006). Gender and age differences in occupational stress and professional burnout between primary and high-school teachers in Greece. *Journal of Managerial Psychology, 21*(7), 682–690.

Bagley, W. C. (1907). *Classroom management.* Norwood, MA: Macmillan.

Barkley, R. (1981). *Hyperactive children.* New York: Guilford Press.

Beane, J. (2005). *A reason to teach.* Portsmouth, NH: Heinemann.

Blase, J., & Kirby, P. (2000). *Bringing out the best in teachers: What effective principals do.* Thousand Oaks, CA: Corwin Press.

Camp, B. W., Blom, G. E., Herbert, F., & Van Doorninck, W. J. (1977) Think aloud: A program for developing self-control in young aggressive boys. *Journal of Abnormal Child Psychology, 5,* 157–169.

Can public learn from private? (1981, April 20). *Time,* 50.

Charles, C. M. (2005). *Building classroom discipline* (8th ed.). Boston: Pearson.

Charles, C. M. (2008). *Today's best classroom management strategies.* Boston: Pearson.

Christian, S. (2003). *Educating children in foster care.* Washington, DC: Children's Policy Initiative. Available: http://www.ncsl.org/programs/cyf/cpieducate.pdf

Ciaccio, J. (2004). *Totally positive teaching.* Alexandria, VA: Association for Supervision and Curriculum Development.

Coloroso, B. (2002). *The bully, the bullied and the bystander.* Toronto: HarperCollins.

Creemers, B. P. M., & Reezigt, G. J. (2005). Linking school effectiveness and school improvement: The background and outline of the project. *School Effectiveness and School Improvement, 16*(4), 359–371.

Crow, K., & Ward-Lonergan, J. (2003). *An analysis of personal event narratives produced by school age children.* Paper presented at the annual meeting of the Council for Exceptional Children, New York. (ERIC Documentation Reproduction Service No. ED 481 292) Retrieved April 10, 2008, from http://www.eric.ed.gov/ERICDocs/data/ericdocs2sql/content_storage_01/0000019b/80/1b/74/98.pdf.

Curwin, R. (1992). *Rediscovering hope: Our greatest teaching strategy.* Bloomington, IN: National Education Service.

Curwin, R. (2003*). Making good choices.* Thousand Oaks, CA: Corwin Press.

Curwin, R. (2006). *Motivating students left behind: Practical strategies for reaching and teaching your most difficult students.* Rochester, NY: Discipline Associates.

Curwin, R., & Mendler, A. (1980). *The discipline book: A complete guide to school and classroom management.* Reston, VA: Reston.

Curwin, R., & Mendler, A. (1999a). *Discipline with dignity* (2nd ed.). Alexandria VA: Association for Supervision and Curriculum Development.

Curwin, R., & Mendler, A. (1999b, October). Zero tolerance for zero tolerance. *Phi Delta Kappan, 119–120.*

Designs for Change. (2005, September 21). 144 Chicago inner city elementary schools serving nearly 100,000 students show 15 years of substantial and sustained achievement gains. Press release. Chicago: Author. Retrieved April 9, 2008, from http://www.designsforchange.org/pdfs/BP_pr_092105.pdf

Driekers, R. (1964). *Children: The challenge.* New York: Hawthorn Books.

Ellis, J., Small-McGinley, J., & De Fabrizio, L. (1999). It's so great to have an adult friend: A teacher-student mentorship program for at-risk youth. *Reaching Today's Youth, 3*(4), 46–50.

Fabiano, G. A., Pelham, P. E., Jr., Gnagy, E. M., Burrows-MacLean, L., Coles, E. K., Chacko, A., et al. (2007). The single and combined effects of multiple intensities of behavior modification and methylphenidate for children with attention deficit hyperactivity disorder in a classroom setting. *School Psychology Review, 36*(2), 195–216.

Feindler, E. L., &. Ecton, R. B. (1986). *Adolescent anger control: Cognitive-behavioral. techniques.* New York: Pergamon.

Fisher, G. (2007, April 9). Amputee looks at his new life as "another chance"; Arizona teacher is inspiration after loss of four limbs. *USA Today,* p. 4D.

Gagnon, C. (2001). *Power cards: Using special interests to motivate children and youth with Asperger Syndrome and autism.* Shawnee Mission, KS: Autism Asperger Publishing.

Gardner, H. (1983). *Frames of mind: The theory of multiple intelligences.* New York: Basic Books.

Gardner, H. (1999). *The disciplined mind: Beyond facts and standardized tests—The K–12 education that every child deserves.* New York: Simon & Schuster.

Goldstein, A. (1999). *The prepared curriculum: Teaching prosocial competencies.* Champaign, IL: Research Press.

Hamilton, B. E., Martin, J. A., & Ventura, S. J. (2006). Births: Preliminary data for 2005. *National Vital Statistics Reports, 55*(11). Retrieved April 9, 2008, from http://www.cdc.gov/nchs/data/nvsr/nvsr55/nvsr55_11.pdf

Henley, M. (2003). *Teaching self control.* Bloomington, IN: Solution Tree.

Hurren, L. (2006). The effects of principals' humor on teachers' job satisfaction. *Educational Studies, 2*(4), 373–385.

Hursh, D., & Ross, E. W. (2000). *Democratic social education: Social studies for social change.* New York: Falmer Press.

Jensen, E. (2000). *Different brains, different learners: How to reach the hard to reach.* Thousand Oaks, CA: Corwin Press.

Keith, S., & Martin, M. (2005). Cyber-bullying: Creating a culture of respect in a cyber world. *Reclaiming Children and Youth, 13*(4), 224.

Larsen, E. (2003). *Violence in U.S. public schools: A summary of findings.* New York: ERIC Clearinghouse on Urban Education, Institute for Urban and Minority Education, Teachers College, Columbia University. (ERIC Documentation Reproduction Service No. ED 482291) Retrieved April 9, 2008, from http://eric.ed.gov/ERICDocs/data/ericdocs2sql/content_storage_01/0000019b/80/1b/99/86.pdf

Levinson, W., & Gallagher, T. H. (2007, July 3.) Disclosing medical errors to patients: A status report in 2007. *Canadian Medical Association Journal 177*(3).

Levinson, W., Roter, D. L., Mullooly, J. P., Dull, V.T., & Frankel, R. M. (1997). Physician-patient communication. *JAMA, 277*(7), 553–559.

Loomans, D., & Kolberg, K. (2002). *The laughing classroom: Everyone's guide to teaching with humor* (2nd ed.). Tiburon, CA: H. J. Kramer; Novato, CA: New World Library.

Loudon, B. J., & McLendon, G. (2007, April 26). City's 39% grad rate worst in Big 4. *Rochester Democrat & Chronicle.* Retrieved April 10, 2008, from www.democratandchronicle.com/apps/pbcs.dll/article?AID=/20070426/NEWS01/704260352

Lundberg, E., & Thurston, C.M. (2002). *If they're laughing they just might be listening: Ideas for using humor effectively in the classroom.* Tiburon, CA: H. J. Kramer.

Lundin, S. C., Christensen, J., & Paul, H. (2002). *Fish tales.* New York: Hyperion.

Marzano, R. (2003) *What works in schools: Translating research into action.* Alexandria, VA: Association for Supervision and Curriculum Development.

Marzano, R. J., & Marzano, J. S. (2003). The key to classroom management. *Educational Leadership, 61*(1), 6–18.

Meichenbaum, D. (1977). *Cognitive behavior modification.* New York: Plenum.

Mendler, A. (1997). *Power struggles: Successful strategies for educators.* Rochester, NY: Discipline Associates.

Mendler, A. (2000). *Motivating students who don't care: Successful techniques for educators.* Bloomington, IN: National Education Service. (ERIC Documentation Reproduction Service No. ED469217)

Mendler, A. (2001). *Connecting with students.* Alexandria VA: Association for Supervision and Curriculum Development.

Mendler, A. (2004). *Just in time: Powerful strategies to promote positive behavior.* Bloomington, IN: National Education Service.

Mendler, A. (2005). *More what do I do when: Powerful strategies to promote positive behavior.* Bloomington, IN: Solution Tree.

Mendler, A. (2006). *Handling difficult parents.* Rochester, NY: Discipline Associates.

Mendler, A. N. & Curwin, R. L. (1999). *Discipline with dignity for challenging youth.* Bloomington, IN: Solution Tree.

Mendler, B., Curwin, R., & Mendler, A. (2008) *Strategies for successful classroom management.* Thousand Oaks, CA: Corwin Press.

MetLife survey. (2004, February 21). *Time,* pp. 40–49.

Molnar, A., & Linquist, B. (1990). *Changing problem behavior in schools.* San Francisco: Jossey-Bass.

Moreno, C., Laje, G., Blanco, C., Jiang, H., Schmidt A. B., & Olfson M. (2007, September). National trends in the outpatient diagnosis and treatment of bipolar disorder in youth. *Archives of General Psychiatry, 64*(9), 1032–1039.

Moscowitz, F., & Hayman J. L. (1974). Interaction patterns of first year, typical and "best" teachers in inner-city schools. *Journal of Educational Research, 67,* 224–230.

MTA Cooperative Group. (2004). National Institute of Mental Health Multimodal Treatment Study of ADHD follow-up: 24-month outcomes of treatment strategies for attention-deficit/hyperactivity disorder. *Pediatrics, 113,* 754–761.

Oliver, K. (2002). Understanding your child's temperament. *Family and Consumer Sciences,* 1–2.

Postlethwaite, T. N., & Ross, K. N. (1992). *Effective schools in reading: Implications for educational planners.* The Hague: International Association for the Evaluation of Educational Achievement. (ERIC Documentation Reproduction Service No. ED 360614) Retrieved April 10, 2008, from http://www.eric.ed.gov/ERICDocs/data/ericdocs2sql/content_storage_01/0000019b/80/13/07/45.pdf

Rogers, S. (1999). *Teaching tips.* Evergreen, CO: Peak Learning Systems.

Rosen, L. (2005). *School discipline.* Thousand Oaks, CA: Corwin Press.

Sigle-Rushton, W., & McLanahan, S. (2002). The living arrangements of new unmarried mothers. *Demography, 39*(3), 415–433.

Smith, R. (2004). *Conscious classroom management.* San Rafael, CA: Conscious Teaching Publications.

Stronge, J. H. (2002). *Qualities of effective teachers.* Alexandria, VA: Association for Supervision and Curriculum Development.

Tomlinson, C. A. (2005). Traveling the road to differentiation in staff development. *Journal of Staff Development, 26*(4).

Tyre, P., Scelfo, J., & Kantrowitz, B. (2004, September 13). *Newsweek,* p. 42.

U.S. Centers for Disease Control and Prevention. (2007, February 8). *CDC releases new data on Autism Spectrum Disorders from multiple communities in the United States.* Press release. Atlanta: Author. Retrieved April 10, 2008, from http://www.cdc.gov/od/oc/media/pressrel/2007/r070208.htm

U.S. Department of Health, Education, and Welfare. (1978). *Violent schools—safe schools: The safe schools report to the Congress, 1978.* Washington, DC: U.S. Government Printing Office. (ERIC Document Reproduction Service No. ED149464)

Van de Grift, W. J. C. M., & Houtveen, A. A. M. (2006). Underperformance in primary schools. *School Effectiveness and School Improvement, 17*(3), 255–273.

Wang, M. C., Haertel, G. D., & Walberg, H. J. (1997). Fostering educational resilience in inner-city schools. *Children and Youth, 7,* 119–140.

Wendt, M. (2002, Fall). Can exercise replace medication as a treatment for ADHD? *Healing Magazine,* 78.

Werner, E. E., & Smith, R.S. (1989). Vulnerable but invincible: A longitudinal study of resilient children and youth. New York: Adams.

White, R., & Lippitt, R. (1960). Leader behavior and member reaction in three "social climates." In D. Cartwright & A . Zander (Eds.), *Group dynamics in researched theory* (2nd ed.). New York: Harper & Row.

Wlodkowski, R. J. (1978). *Motivation and teaching: A practical guide.* Washington, DC: National Education Association.

Wong, H. K., & Wong. R. T. (2004). *The first days of school: How to be an effective teacher* (3rd ed.). Mountain View, CA: Harry K. Wong Publications.

❦ Index ❦

The letter *f* following a page number denotes a figure.

❧ About the Authors ❧

Richard L. Curwin, Ph.D., is an author, speaker, and experienced practitioner who explores issues of student discipline, behavioral management, and motivation. Having served as a 7th grade educator, teacher of emotionally disturbed children, and college professor, Dr. Curwin has a breadth of experience in the classroom. The behavior management strategies and philosophies he shares with educators have worked for him. Dr. Curwin and his colleague Dr. Allen N. Mendler founded Discipline Associates and created the Discipline with Dignity program. Dr. Curwin coauthored *Discipline with Dignity for Challenging Youth* and *As Tough as Necessary: Countering Violence, Aggression, and Hostility in Our Schools.* He is also the author of *Making Good Choices* and *Motivating Students Left Behind.* Dr. Curwin's latest video set, *The Four Keys to Effective Classroom and Behavior Management,* which he developed with Dr. Mendler and Brian Mendler, won the 2007 Association of Educational Publishers Distinguished Achievement Award in School/Class Management-Technology.

Allen N. Mendler, Ph.D., is an educator and school psychologist who has worked extensively with children of all ages in regular education and special education settings. Dr. Mendler's emphasis is on developing effective frameworks and strategies for educators, youth professionals, and parents to help difficult youth succeed. He has written a number of books, including *Motivating Students Who Don't Care, Connecting with Students, What Do I Do When, Power Struggles: Successful Techniques for Educators*, and *Handling Difficult Parents*. He recently co-authored *Strategies for Successful Classroom Management*. Dr. Mendler was the recipient of The Spirit of Crazy Horse Award in recognition of his lifelong contribution to improving the lives of challenging youth.

Brian D. Mendler is a recognized authority on behavior and classroom management. The strategies he shares with K–12 teachers and administrators are the same ones he uses in his own classrooms with great success. Brian is a certified elementary and special education teacher with extensive experience working with challenging students in general education, self-contained, and inclusion classrooms. He continues to be a highly sought after consultant and has worked extensively throughout the United States, Canada, and England. Brian is also an adjunct professor at St. John Fisher College in Rochester, N.Y., where he teaches Behavior Management. Brian continues to volunteer in the Big Brothers Big Sisters program and with the Special Olympics.

Related ASCD Resources: Discipline

At the time of publication, the following ASCD resources were available (ASCD stock numbers appear in parentheses). For up-to-date information about ASCD resources, go to www.ascd.org.

Networks

Visit the ASCD Web site (www.ascd.org) and search for "networks" for information about professional educators who have formed groups around topics like "Affective Factors in Learning," and "Authentic Assessment." Look in the "Network Directory" for current facilitators' addresses and phone numbers.

Online Courses

Classroom Management: A Teacher-Student Collaboration (#07OC65)
Managing Challenging Behavior (#05OC46)

Print Products

Beyond Discipline: From Compliance to Community by Alfie Kohn (#106033)
The Educator's Guide to Assessing and Improving School Discipline Programs by Mark Boynton and Christine Boynton (#107073)
Totally Positive Teaching: A Five-Stage Approach to Energizing Students and Teachers by Joseph Ciaccio (#104016)
Educating Oppositional and Defiant Children by Philip S. Hall and Nancy D. Hall (# 901061)

For more information: send e-mail to member@ascd.org; call 1-800-933-2723 or 703-578-9600, press 2; send a fax to 703-575-5400; or write to Information Services, ASCD, 1703 N. Beauregard St., Alexandria, VA 22311-1714 USA.